P9-DWI-633

MY DRUNK KITCHEN

HOLIDAYS!

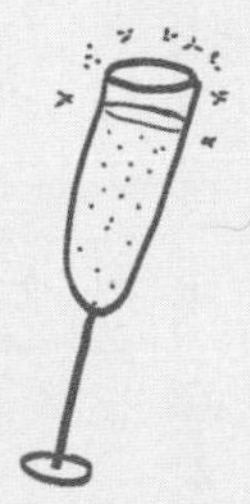

ALSO BY HANNAH HART

My Drunk Kitchen: A Guide to Eating, Drinking, and Going with Your Gut

Buffering: Unshared Tales of a Life Fully Loaded

MY DRUNK KITCHEN

HOLIDAYS!

HOW TO SAVOR AND CELEBRATE THE YEAR

HANNAH HART

An imprint of Penguin Random House LLC
penguinrandomhouse.com

Photographs by Dane Tashima Photography

Photographs on pages 164 and 167 by Maxwell Poth

Screenshots on pages 62 and 63 courtesy of the author

Doodles by Hannah Hart and Kelly Diamond, Shutterstock, and Lorie Pagnozzi

Library of Congress Cataloging-in-Publication Data
Names: Hart, Hannah, 1986– author.
Title: My drunk kitchen holidays! : how to savor and celebrate the year / Hannah Hart.
Description: First edition. | New York : Plume, 2019.
Identifiers: LCCN 2019022580 | ISBN 9780525541431 (hardback) | ISBN 9780525541448 (ebook)
Subjects: LCSH: Holiday cooking. | LCGFT: Cookbooks.
Classification: LCC TX739 .H37 2019 | DDC 641.5/68—dc23
LC record available at https://lccn.loc.gov/2019022580

Printed in the United States of America
10 9 8 7 6 5 4 3 2 1

Book design by Lorie Pagnozzi

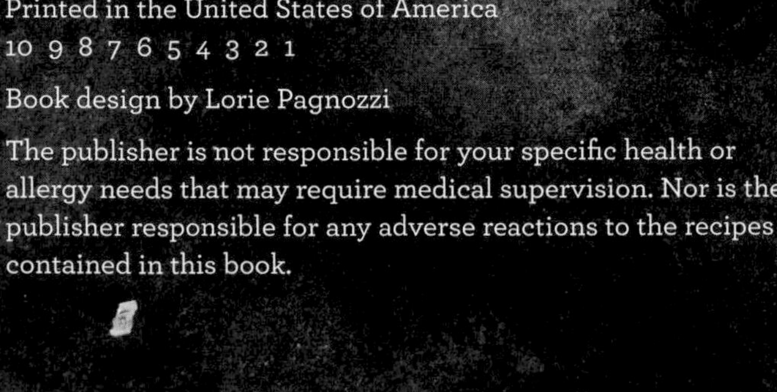

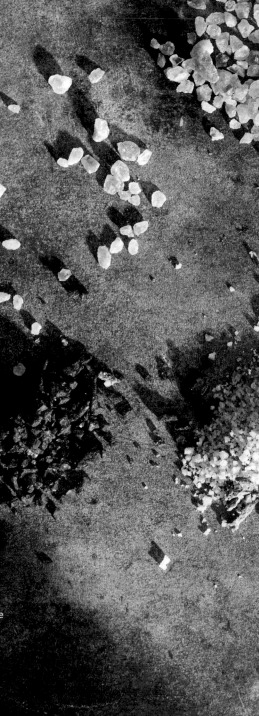

TO ALL OUR SIBLINGS,
WHO TAUGHT US HOW
TO CELEBRATE, SAVOR,
AND SURVIVE.

CONTENTS

ER WATE

INTRODUCTION

Dear Hannah,

I can't believe you've written your third book! This has been a hard one, huh? That's okay. You've only just learned how to savor and celebrate the year, so it's pretty ambitious of you to think you could teach others to do the same. But what's another word for "ambition"? "Arrogance." Just kidding. Wow. Don't take yourself too seriously over there, kiddo. You may be thirty-two and have two other books under your belt, but every creative craft is different. Especially this one.

Remember when you wrote your first book? *My Drunk Kitchen: A Guide to Eating, Drinking, and Going with Your Gut*—that seems like so long ago now, doesn't it? Over two hundred pages of heartfelt gibberish and photos taken in an apartment you lived in for less than a year. And recipes that some people actually wanted to make! Wild. It's even more wild to think that you've signed copies of that book for the last six years since it was published. Six years! Congratulations, buddy.

Oh, and then you wrote *Buffering: Unshared Tales of a Life Fully Loaded*—that was a doozy, wasn't it? A book that surmised your entire life to date. An autobiography. The book you've always wanted to write about homelessness, and family, and love, and mental health. The book that took years off your life and then put them back on. A book made from equal parts tears and joy. A book that showed you so much shared community that you never knew how to find but always wanted. Remem ber the day the book came out and you cried the whole plane ride home—reading the reviews online *and* in the *New York Times*? Holy hell, Hannah! There's a lot to be proud of, isn't there?

Oh, what's that?

You don't know how to be proud?

You don't know how to slow down and take it all in?

Or even pat yourself on the back for a job well done?

Well, you're in luck cuz this book is for YOU!

Over the last few years, I've spent a lot of time celebrating. Books, movies, TV shows, etc. There's been a lot to do. Now that all the above has slowed down (for the time being!), there's not much left to celebrate, is there? WRONG. There's a LOT to celebrate. And you can celebrate all year long!

The Holidays (capital *H* for the big ones) can be equal parts exhilirating and exhausting. And that's not really fair considering it's your chance to let loose and take a break. That got me thinking . . . is there a smaller way to savor and celebrate all year long? That way, the months prior to "The Holidays" don't have to be a constant trudge toward obligatory hosting and family time. How do you even host something, anyway? And why do you love your family so much but feel so drained after seeing them?

This book seeks to answer all those questions and more. And to give some shout-outs and recognition to the lesser holidays that so often get passed over. Holidays like:

Middle Child's Day!

Left-Hander's Day!

Just Get Over It Day!

Be a Millionaire Day!

. . . And so many more!

It's pretty cool that you've written another cookbook to pass along some tips and tricks to others. You're pretty lucky to get to attend a lot of celebrations throughout the year. Now, your job is to share that with others and keep the party going! (In a refreshing and relaxing way, of course.)

So let's take a look at how you did, shall we? I really hope this book doesn't suck. I've been looking forward to reading it. Even if it did suck, the act of writing it and finishing it is definitely something worth celebrating. So let's bust open a bottle, baby. Don't save champagne.

Love,
Hannah

P.S. For real, though . . . I hope this book is good.

MY DRUNK KITCHEN

HOLIDAYS!

JANUARY

HERE WE GO AGAIN! WHO'S READY FOR ANOTHER TRIP AROUND THE SUN? I KNOW I AM!

Or rather, I know that I can be . . .

Welcome to January! An arbitrary start point for all your anxiety for the year ahead! For those of you in school, this is in the middle of your year. For those of you who work full-time jobs, this is . . . another month! Because guess what, kids—after you're out of school, there is no Summer™ anymore! And it sucks! Trust me. This is coming from someone old who still calls the end of December "Winter Break."

January is the month where you begin (and end) all your resolutions for the self that you seek to be. But why so much pressure? What a rough way to start the year! Instead of chastising yourself for the things you didn't do, let's look at all the things you did.

You survived last year.

. . . And maybe that's it!

But that's still pretty great! There's nothing I want more from my time on this earth than to help turn your surviving into thriving. And what better way to do that than by sharing a bunch of nonsense (and semi-nonsense) recipes in celebration of many minor moments, reveling in holidays as obscure as Eat What You Want Day and as familiar as New Year's Day and many more in between?

There's always cause for celebration. There are always moments to savor. Which is why you're here. And also why I gave the book that really classy subtitle. Wow. You've got some great taste.

Ahem. Back to January itself!

The following holidays and recipes are here to help ease you into the next 365 days of your life. We are gonna start with a little Motivation to put some pep in your step and end with some Acceptance to be the insole that supports your arches* so you can keep your steps full of pep all year round.

* Anybody else have one leg shorter than the other? Damn these childbearing hips! Constantly falling out of sync with each other!

≫ NEW YEAR'S DAY: 1/1 ≪

HELLO! Welcome to this year! It's good to see you here! Shall we party?

Ah, New Year's. To be honest, this is one of my favorite holidays. Well, it's one of my favorite holidays to host and celebrate in the privacy of my own home. Future Bride ("fiancée" is such an awkward term) Ella also loves to host, and thus we are getting married. (And some other reasons too, I'm sure.)

New Year's is a time of resolution and resignation. A time of reflection. A time of inspection. A time of detection . . . as in detecting how many more decibels you can turn up Toto's "Africa" before the cops come and start issuing noise complaints. The answer is six.

New Year's can also be a time of unnecessary self-beratement. Looking back on the year behind you and searching for something that's missing can be really defeating. Instead I think it's important to look back and pick out your favorite moments, or the things you were most proud of, and then simply try to increase those moments in the year ahead. This will take a fair amount of personal understanding and forgiveness. Flexibility, even.

Once you understand what you want going forward (or rather what you want *more often*), the next step is understanding what's standing in the way of that. For me, it's about momentum and motivation. I don't know why or how, but I've fully tricked myself into believing that the *thinking* of the thing is just as satisfying as the actual *doing* of the thing.

→ **EXAMPLE: Man, I had the best time taking those boxing classes (twice). I want to do it more often! I'm going to sign up for a boxing membership! Then I'm sure I'll go more often!**

Seems convincing enough. And probably executable, right?

Wrong.*

Sure, signing up for a boxing membership would be motivating if the thought of losing the money on the membership would scare me into going. But fear doesn't motivate me. Or maybe I think the shame of not showing up to the classes will motivate me into it. Nope. Shame doesn't motivate me either. In fact, it's more likely to keep me as far away from the boxing gym as possible. If anything, it will lead me to avoid the place for fear of the perceived disappointment in the eyes of the receptionist.

So if negative consequences don't motivate me . . . if convenience and accessibility don't motivate me . . . then what does?

The answer for me? Carbs. Not just any carbs, though. Truly excellent carbs. A basket full of baked goods is my reward for the discipline it takes for a job well done.

* For me! Disclaimer: Everything in this book is pretty much centered around me, so be open to interpretation and how things apply to you.

MY BREAD BASKET OF BLISS

INGREDIENTS

Fancy basket and assorted pastries . . . some of my personal favorites include:

- sourdough bread
- Pain au chocolat
- cinnamon rolls

Sourdough bread is a form of comfort food for me. Grill it, add a layer of butter, watch it melt, wait for a little char, add some salt, watch it dissolve, and then dissolve yourself into a state of carby-buttery bliss.

Pain au chocolat is my favorite "job well done" treat. Answered three hundred e-mails? Well, guess who is getting a baked good! And that little burst of caffeine in the chocolate just might make you eager to answer three hundred more.

Cinnamon rolls are one of the greatest gifts the universe has given humanity. Have you ever had a fresh-baked cinnamon roll? Have you ever tried to make one from scratch? I think that baking a cinnamon roll is a great and approachable challenge for when you want to zone out and immerse yourself in an activity outside of life.

Don't know where to start? Here is the same sentiment repeated as a list. Just for those of you who are always skimming for the TL;DR version of life.

1. Reflect on the year. Think about the things you felt proud of and would like to do more often.
2. Determine your personal roadblock.
3. Determine your personal reward . . . block.
4. Do the thing! Reward yourself with bread, or whatever your personal poison might be.
5. Repeat and apply every twelve months.

pyrex
Sugar
PURE CANE SUGAR
IMPERIAL
GRANULATED
AZUCAR GRANULADA

TRIVIA DAY: 1/4

AT THE NEXT STOP IN OUR JANUARY OF JUBILATION, WE ARE GOING TO CELEBRATE THE MIND BY FILLING IT WITH KNOWLEDGE! That's right—we are celebrating Trivia Day.

So, in honor of Trivia Day, I'd like to play a quick game with you. A trivia game! Consisting of one statement: The earth is flat (T/F).

False! (Currently.)

See, even though the ancient Greeks first theorized that the earth was a sphere, the theory didn't gain momentum until the Middle Ages. Previously, those who *contested* the "truth" of the flat earth were deemed heretics. Today, they are lauded as revolutionaries. Also today, the idea of a flat earth is beginning anew. Right up there with people who deny the existence of anything microscopic.

So as you can tell, "truth" is often up for debate.

• • •

Which brings me to the subject of juice. When I first moved to Los Angeles, not only was I introduced to the existence of something called "kale," but I was also introduced to an industry all its own known as "Juice." Now "Juice" comes in many forms. There's cold-pressed . . . um . . . hot-pressed? . . . Sometimes juice is even blue algae from a lake. And yes, we still call *that* Juice.

The discussion of the health benefits in Juice hinges on one crucial factor: sugar. What's so bad about sugar anyway?

WELL, BUCKLE UP BECAUSE I'M ABOUT TO TELL YA.

"Sugar" can be a very fast-burning and easily accessible source of energy. That's not so bad, right? After all, food is meant to be fuel for the body.

Sugar can only function as this great gift to the body if it has its companion *fiber*. I'm not going to get too deep into the nitty-gritty, but that's what you need to know. Sugar + Fiber = useful for the body. Sugar sans Fiber = empty. Thus becoming storage for the body, aka fat.

Alternatively: A store-bought juice can contain as much sugar as a soda. Let that sink in for a second. As much sugar as a SODA. That's a lot!

But, Hannah, how are we supposed to get our vitamins and nutrients if something as innocent as juice can be so deceptive?

Well, frankly . . . by eating fruit. All the missing pieces we get from drinking a juice come together as a whole in one perfectly assembled, portable, self-contained, prewrapped organic being. Fruit! You don't need plastic to keep your orange fresh. All you need to do is eat it within its life span. Accept that all things are temporary, even this delicious tiny ball of sunrise. It will rot someday. So might as well give it the chance to live up to its purpose.

WARNING: THIS WILL INVOLVE CLEANING THE JUICER.

However, if you really wanna juice, here is a juice that I would happily consume . . . because you're gonna be sharing some with me, right? Listen, I have a juicer, but it's still in its box, so I'm gonna have to come over to yours.

JUICE DON'T WORRY ABOUT IT

INGREDIENTS

Ginger

Lemon

Orange

Turmeric

Oregano oil

Cayenne

A deep breath

1. Determine whether you want to clean a juicer at the end of this. If you've got that kind of stamina, then the steps are to simply put all that stuff in a juicer and then drink it. Be *very* sparing with the oregano oil. That shit burns.

Don't have a juicer? Fear not! Here is how you do it *a mano*:

2. Peel and grate your ginger into a cheesecloth. Squeeze the remnants into a cup. Be both frustrated and disappointed by the amount of juice all the effort provided.

3. Reflect on this moment next time you're at a juicery and think about how much work the staff has to go through to make your bottled and blended drinks.

4. Put your ginger juice into a shot glass so it seems like more than it is.

5. Squeeze a lemon into the same glass.

6. Squeeze an orange into the same glass.

7. Add a dash of turmeric.

8. Add a dash of cayenne.

9. Add the TINIEST AMOUNT OF OREGANO OIL. This stuff is no joke. You're gonna be smelling like a pizza for the rest of the day if you add too much.

10. Take a picture of your healthy shot and post it to Instagram, because damn, girl, you're good.

11. Take the shot. Live forever.

Now get ready for the rest of the month because January ain't over yet! Glad you're off to a healthy start because this year has just begun . . .

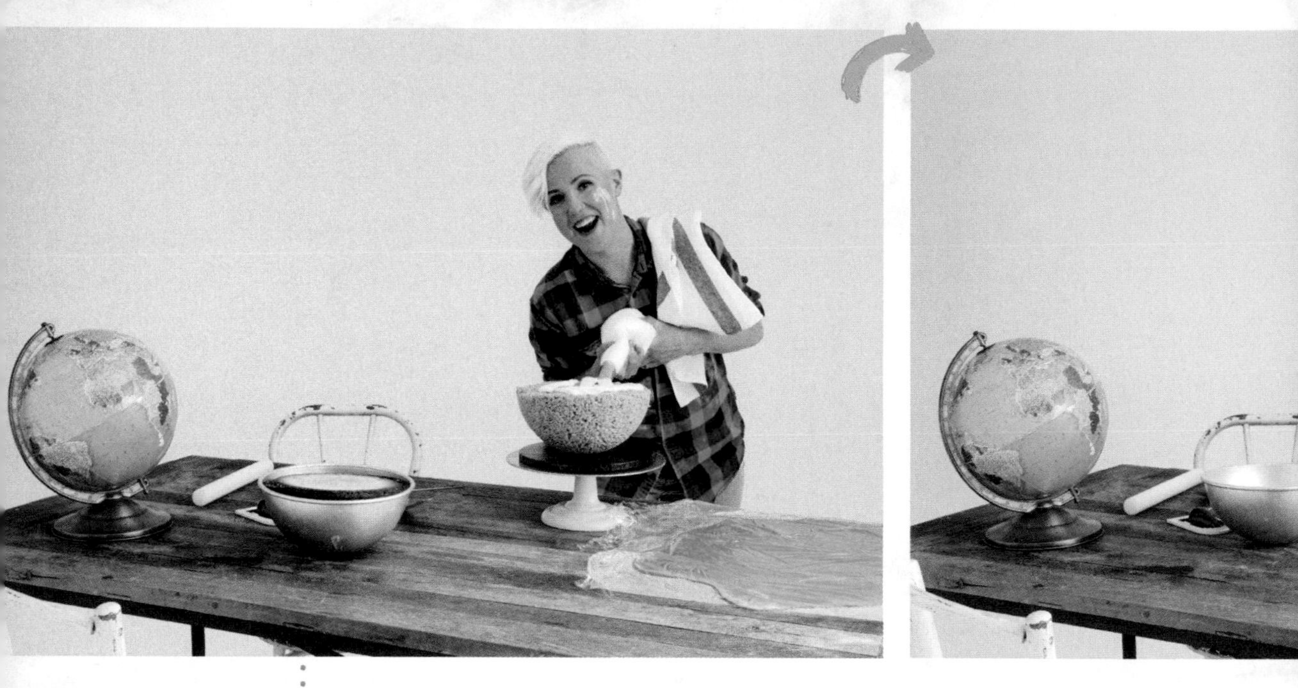

PLAY GOD DAY: 1/9

SOMETIMES THE PERSON SITTING NEXT TO ME ON A FLIGHT CROSSES THEMSELVES RIGHT BEFORE TAKE-OFF. I always look to see if they are wearing a cross, or reading some Christian novel, or if they have one of those wrist bands that says things like Jesus Loves You or some other variation of Christian identifier.

In those moments, I'm always tempted to be like, "Does that balance out my sin? Just in case my homo status is the thing that brings this plane down."

And then I smack myself mentally for being so judgmental. Because there are tons of Christian denominations out there that embrace the rainbow, so why should I assume that this

middle-aged white lady with the big hair is some sort of closeted bigot? That's not very godly of me. And if anything, their faith is meant to be the way that they find their guidance in a world that seems so thoroughly lacking of moral principle. Though, many of the people in power lacking those principles are self-avowed Christians so . . . well, now I'm back to square one.

Flying over the country, I can't help but think about how much space there is between people. If you look at a map of America's population, you'll notice how spread out the states can be. There are miles and miles between families, and many more miles (mental miles, philosophical miles) between cultures. America is such a weird place.

But America isn't the whole world. There's the rest of the globe out there, and those other countries have just as many opinions and perspectives as we do. We should probably study the histories of others as much as we study the history of ourselves, because our nation is so young that it's going to have to learn every lesson as we go. The danger is that we are also a very powerful country. So if we are going to learn that the stove is hot by touching it . . . well, maybe we should skip that lesson altogether and look at the social/civil disruptions in other nations and try to avoid it on our own.

And then I wonder, where's God in all this?

I wish I believed in God the way I did when I was growing up. There is nothing more comforting than a sense of purpose, the idea of reason, the thought that maybe all those people out there suffering at the hands of hate will wake up somewhere better than they were before. How does God make decisions? How would I make decisions if I were God?

Believe it or not, as I wrapped my arms around this cake, I was wondering about the meaning of it all and our relationship to this giant spinning rock hurtling through space at an inconceivable pace.

Then I realized that our relationship to this rock mirrors our relationship with God itself. It all depends on our relationships with one another.

Jesus says, "Do unto others."

The planet says, "Y'all better rely on each other because IDGAF about you and I'm gonna be whatever I am until I eventually explode."

Somewhere in that I hope to find some comfort in accepting our shared experience of humanity. "Playing God" with the only lives we are given. Every day deciding what kind of Creator we'll be.

GLOBE CAKE

INGREDIENTS

2 Half-dome cakes

Frosting

Blue and green fondant

1. Ask a baker you know to bake you (or teach you how to bake) a cake that's two separate half domes you can merge into one.

2. Marry the two halves together with a thick layer of frosting.

3. Roll out dark blue fondant, and very gently wrap it around the marvel of your creation.

4. Cut out vaguely continental shapes from green fondant, and stick them arbitrarily on top of your sugary sea. Or stick them with a lot of thought and attention. Depends on what kind of God you are.

5. Finish and walk away. Hope it finds its purpose in this life. But know for the most part, that little globe is on its own.

VISION BOARD DAY:

SECOND SATURDAY OF THE MONTH

I DON'T BELIEVE IN A FIVE-YEAR PLAN. So much can change in five years! Health, marriages, presidencies, not to mention the entire media industry. The list goes on. I've always felt that having a five-year plan is a little too "center of the universe-y" for my taste. Frankly, the people I know who've had five-year plans are the people who have the most emotionally volatile responses to things that change—to the unforeseen in general. The people with the tightest plans sometimes haven't planned for disappointment if things don't pan out. So, in my opinion, it's much better to be flexible when it comes to the "plan" and instead to focus your energy on achieving the **"goal."**

What's the difference between a five-year goal and a five-year plan? Well, it's a big one! A plan is a sense of security in an otherwise unknown future. It's lovely, but its execution alone isn't what you're trying to achieve. The best-laid plans are the ones with goals in mind. So why not just focus on the

goal itself and leave the plan open to change? For instance, let's say you have a five-year goal of moving out of your parents' house. That's a big goal! That's a great goal! That's a goal that's going to take some effort to achieve. And if you've spent all your energy mapping out a plan that is dependent on itself for success, well, what happens if the first step doesn't go well? Does the whole plan fall apart?

Meanwhile, someone with a goal will be able to turn and pivot with the times. Need to move out? Okay, then you need to save money. Start saving money. Doesn't matter so much how, just that you do it. (I recommend putting 30 percent of every paycheck into savings.) Don't know how much to save? Well, do a little research and find out. All this is achievable because there is no timeline; there is only the end result.

SO, IF YOU (LIKE ME) HAVE FELT INFERIOR FOR NOT HAVING A "PLAN," THEN TRY OUT HAVING A "GOAL" INSTEAD.

From that point on it's up to you to achieve it. So start moving in the direction of it, because everything changes constantly. You're welcome, and good luck!

• • •

Today as we celebrate Vision Board Day, we are going to follow a recipe for making something (anything!) to practice thinking about the things we want. Enjoy!

V IS FOR VISIONARY

INGREDIENTS

Bottle of wine (come on, this is how all good brainstorms start)

A paper crown (because you're taking charge!)

Poster paper (or any paper)

Some sort of glue

Assorted food items

1. Invite your least judgmental and most fun-loving friends over. People who are good at nonsense and conversation.

2. Or not! Maybe this is a solo act. You do you.

3. Lay out a large piece of paper, assorted food items, and get started. Which is the first item that compels you? Start there! Start gluing that item to as many places as you want!

4. Not feeling creative yet? Take a drink!

5. Open up a magazine and look at the things those shiny people have. Is there anything in there you'd like to have too? Health insurance, perhaps? Great! Glue on some cough drops into the shape of a flower. Now you'll remember to start exploring your options!

6. Need money to have health insurance? No problem! Open up some instant coffee and sprinkle it on the bottom of your board. These caffeine pellets represent your motivation to get a job so your cough drop sunshine flower (aka health insurance) can bloom beautifully.

7. Think your pic still looks a little empty? Draw faces or symbols on some marshmallows and put them in the sky. These can be the "nice things" you'll add to your board after you've achieved your health insurance goal . . .

8. . . . And so on.

The point of a goal is not to overwhelm yourself with a plan. It's just to get started. When you begin with the first step, you'll soon find yourself with a lot of other things to figure out. Remind yourself that that's okay. And that's what this exercise is for . . . figuring it out, and allowing yourself to have some fun while you do it.

ချစ်ခြင်းမေတ္တာ

PRĪTI

FEB-

ANPU

प्रेम

PRĒMA

AMOUR

любов

애정

SNĒHAM

RU-

ความรัก

AMOR

愛

मोहब्बत

LIEBE

TRESNA

محبت

ARY

AMORE

YÊU

ভালবাসা

عشق

PASADA HAI

ప్రేమ

OR . . . . . . LOVE.

LOVE! LOVE LOVE LOVE. The words to the left all mean love. And February is the month we choose to celebrate love the most! Which is kind of silly because . . . Christmas wasn't that long ago . . . and I'm pretty sure that's another great time to show someone how much you love them. Especially if Gifts is your love language.*

But what does *Love* mean to *You*? Well, love can mean many different things. And there are many different types of love! According to the ancient Greeks, there are at least EIGHT different types of love!

THEY ARE

Eros: erotic love / desire / the way I look at a croissant

Philia: affectionate love / platonic / the way I look at a bagel

Storge: familiar love / nostalgia / the way I look at Bagel Bites

Ludus: playful love / euphoria / the way I look at Red Bull

Mania: obsessive love / obsession / the way I look at cheese

Pragma: enduring love / mature / the way I look at aged cheese

Philautia: self-love / healthful / the way I look at water

Agape: selfless love / altruism / the way I look at . . . a . . . grape . . . ey . . . Get it? Agape? A grape? Does that work? NVM.

The ancient Greeks did a lot of cool stuff, and coming up with eight different ways to explain love is one of them! But once you've determined what kind of love you're vibing on . . . how do you sustain it? How do you ignite those passions? How do you awaken the taste buds of your soul into another year of experience and experimentation?

LET'S FIND OUT!

* Referring to the Five Love Languages: Words of Affirmation (saying positive things, writing love notes, etc.), Acts of Service (do the dishes, dammit!), Gifts (favorite pens are always a welcome gift), Quality Time (quality time means facing each other, not facing a screen together), and Physical Touch (hugs, cuddles, sexy times).

ER WATER
Chocolate cupcake with chocolate frosting, crushed dried strawberries, and rose petals
Vanilla cupcake with buttercream, berries, and gold luster dust
Roasted tomato with goat cheese frosting, bacon, and thyme (cornbread cupcake)
Lemon cupcake with lemon buttercream and edible flowers
Cornbread with savory cream cheese frosting, herbs, lemon zest, caper berries, and rainbow radish

VALENTINE'S DAY: 2/14

AH, CUPCAKES. Tiny cakes of cup. I don't particularly like cupcakes because they all taste the same and I tend to be a person who favors the savory side of life. But there's a way to make savory cupcakes! With blue cheese, even!

• • •

My Future Bride, Ella, and I fought a lot in the first year of our relationship. We had a lot of arguments about things like taxes and Santa Claus. We are both very stubborn people, and we both think ourselves to be the ones who are right.

Ella and I improved a lot in the first year of our relationship as well. We encouraged each other to move in the direction of our goals. I helped her unlock her fears around financial planning. She helped me learn to be more direct in asking for what I want. Without this mix of tenderness and toughness, I don't think we would have been able to overcome our doubts and deepen our trust. Trust has to be tested. That's how you know it's more than words.

So, like these cupcakes, our relationship has been a mix of sweet and savory. Love is beautiful because it challenges you and forces you to grow—falling deeper in love with yourself as well as with your partner.

SWEET AND SAVORY CUPCAKES

INGREDIENTS

Box of cupcake mix / box of cornbread mix

Store-bought frosting / blue cheese + cream cheese

SWEET CUPCAKES

1. Make a cupcake. Put frosting on top. This isn't the interesting part to me. This next part is!

SAVORY CUPCAKES

1. Make a cornbread mix. Bake like a cupcake. It's that simple!

2. Then make a blue cheese frosting, which involves the following:

3. Combine blue cheese with cream cheese—blend together and taste often. Maybe even using a cracker. It's just that good.

4. Taste and season with salt and peps.

5. Put it in a piping bag and pipe onto cornbread cupcakes. Make sure you're piping it onto the right batch! This will not taste good over a sweet cupcake.

6. Adorn with blue cheese crumbles or maybe just a tiny sign warning your guests that this is more of an appetizer and less of a dessert. I find that people like a little heads-up when it comes to the foods they are eating.

Cupcakes are like tiny celebrations all on their own. It's like handing someone a cake that's all for them. A world of celebration they don't have to share. Personally, I find sharing to be the best part of celebrations, but I know for some of us, feeling special is the exception to the rule. I wish everyone felt special every day. Your life is special because it's yours and no one else's. So whether you choose to celebrate Valentine's with yourself, with your lover, or with your friends, know that the choice is yours to make. And if you are debating between a sweet or savory cupcake . . . well, then, that choice is yours to make too. Or rather, yours to . . . bake. *BA DUM BUM.*

FUN FACT: IT TAKES FOURTEEN
TO EIGHTEEN MONTHS TO GROW
A SINGLE CALIFORNIA AVOCADO.
—CALIFORNIA AVOCADO
COMMISSION

SINGLES AWARENESS DAY: 2/15

I'VE NEVER LIKED THE PHRASE "GOOD THINGS COME TO THOSE WHO WAIT." It leaves me feeling empty and impatient. Every time someone tells me that, a sense of helplessness sparks within me. I appreciate the thought. The idea that patience will proffer its own reward is a lovely sentiment. But it doesn't click. Maybe I need a more grounded example—something to symbolize the "good things" that will "come" after "waiting." Without one, it's hard to get a sense of the weight behind the words.

What are the "good things"? A romantic partner? Or is it a personal goal? A professional one? I've seen friends run the corporate track waiting for the recognition of their efforts, and if that recognition doesn't come, then does that mean that they don't get any good things?

And what about the idea that good things are going to "come" and appear before you? What's taking them so long? What are the good things off doing out there in the world?

And then there is the waiting. For me, "wait" is one of the most active verbs. To wait is to ruminate. To wait is to subjugate (yourself). Waiting is a skill, in my opinion. Being patient allows you to sit in a state of being. To be patient you must become patient. Being patient can be practiced. Waiting implies anticipation, which to me is the opposite of acceptance.

Now, are you ready for me to blow your mind? The maxim actually stems from a poem. And it's not "good things"; it's "all things."

And guess what? The poem doesn't have a happy ending. As it was written by Lady Mary Montgomerie Currie in the nineteenth century:

Ah! "All things come to those who wait"—
(I say these words to make me glad).
But something answers soft and sad—
"They come, but often come too late!"

The poem is essentially about a missed connection. About two people whose love for each other never timed up right. She loved him, but he wasn't interested. When he gained interest, she lost hers. One (or both) of them had in fact been waiting too long. The timing never worked out.

Now you could look at this and say, "See, but if they had just waited, their love *would* have lined up correctly!" To this I'd like to say nay.* Their love wasn't meant to be because the timing didn't work out. You can't wait for someone else's rejection to spur their epiphany. In fact, you can't wait for someone else's anything at all!

Again, waiting is not the same as being patient. Being patient means that you understand and acknowledge why the delay is necessary. It's similar to mutual love or affection. Agreed upon by both parties.

Waiting is anticipation. And anticipation is the opposite of acceptance.

* Sorry, been reading too much nineteenth-century poetry.

• • •

So next time someone is encouraging you to just sit back and wait, remember the California avocado. Remember the fourteen to eighteen months it took to lead to that moment of consumption. Don't be too eager. Don't be too shy. Accept the timing it takes to get the things you want.

Making my favorite avocado toast is pretty simple, but it will take you more than zero seconds in the morning, so it's best to time it and not to rush. You deserve at least thirty minutes for your first meal of the day, right? It'll only take five minutes to make it, but if you want to enjoy it, you're gonna need to slow down.

ACCEPTANCE AVOCADO TOAST

INGREDIENTS

1 appropriately-waited-for California avocado

Garlic-infused olive oil

Lemon

Sea salt

Cracked red pepper

Your favorite kind of toasty toast

1. Cut the avocado in half and admire the perfect circle of the pit. You'll know you've timed it right when the pit looks smooth and dark. There shouldn't be a bunch of avocado residue on it—that means the avocado wasn't ready to let go.

2. Scoop half out into a small, stylish bowl. You're making avocado toast, dammit. Gotta look good while doing it.

3. Add lemon. I like a truly excessive amount of lemon in my life. I love the color. I love the acid. I just love this citrus so damn much. If you're feeling like you want texture, you can even zest a little of the lemon into it, but that's a move you can make later on. For now you just wanna try to make this tasty thing.

4. Add sea salt to taste. Maybe throw some black pepper in there if ya want.

5. Drizzle a small amount of garlic-infused olive oil and mush it all together. The olive oil will help the avocado become creamy and more accepting of the other flavors you've added. If you feel like it's more clunky than creamy, either add more oil or just deal with it and move on. Nobody's perfect. Not even avocados.

6. Toss a pinch of cracked red pepper on top and call it a day. Or rather, start your day. This is a breakfast food, dammit, and I just want to make sure you guys get a chance to know how tasty a semi-hasty breakfast can be.

IT BEARS NOTING THAT THE AVOCADO PICTURED ON THE PREVIOUS PAGE BEARS LITTLE RESEMBLANCE TO THE ONE YOU'VE JUST ASSEMBLED. THINK OF IT MORE LIKE A MOVIE POSTER OF THE ELEMENTS INVOLVED. THIS PICTURE MAKES ME FEEL GOOD AND GRATEFUL FOR AVOS AND ALL THEY PROVIDE. I HOPE IT MAKES YOU FEEL THIS WAY TOO.

DRINK WINE DAY: 2/18

WHEN I THINK OF DRINKING WINE, I THINK OF EATING PASTA. So to celebrate Drink Wine Day, I'd like to share with you some simple facts about cooking pasta. It's easy, but it does involve a little more attention than you'd think. Pasta is part of a process. There are many parts to pasta that make the whole. I was fortunate enough to have an absolutely lovely working relationship with Barilla pasta, and their Italian chefs taught me things that have changed my approach to pasta forever.

If I had to boil it all down,* I would say pasta comes down to these steps:

SIMPLE PASTA AND WINE

DIFFERENT TYPES OF PASTA HAVE DIFFERENT COOK TIMES. YOU CAN FIND THE ALLOTTED TIME ON THE SIDE OF THE BOX.

SALT YOUR WATER. *IT SHOULD TASTE LIKE THE ADRIATIC SEA.*

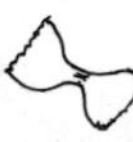

DEPENDING ON WHAT SHAPE OF PASTA YOU WANT TO MAKE, FACTOR IN A LITTLE LESS TIME ON THE BOIL TO GIVE YOU TIME TO FINISH COOKING IT IN THE PAN WITHOUT OVERCOOKING IT.

WHEN YOU'VE REACHED AN AL DENTE THAT YOU'RE COMFORTABLE WITH, DON'T DUMP OUT THE WATER.

TRANSFER YOUR PASTA FROM THE POT TO THE PAN WHERE YOU'VE GOT YOUR OLIVE OIL AND FLAVOR FRIENDS WAITING.

IF YOU'RE THINKING THINGS LOOK A LITTLE DRY OR MAYBE YOU'RE WORRIED YOUR PASTA ISN'T COOKED ENOUGH, DON'T PANIC. SIMPLY LADLE SOME OF YOUR STARCHY GLORY ONTO THE PAN. OH, THE STARCHY GLORY IS THE WATER YOU'VE GOT LEFT OVER FROM THE INITIAL BOIL.

* PUN INTENDED.

ONCE YOU'RE SATISFIED, ADD YOUR MORE FRAGILE FLAVOR FRIENDS. YOUR CHEESE OR YOUR FRESH HERBS. MAYBE A SLICED CHERRY TOMATO. THESE ARE THE THINGS THAT GO ON AT THE END. THE FRESHNESS WILL BRING A QUALITY OF LIFE TO YOUR PASTA.

When I think of pasta, I think of family. I think of it as one of the best ways of sharing a meal while allowing each other to have our differences. Try a pasta night where you let everyone add their own spin—meaning putting things in their own bowls. Slice up the herbs, blanch some veggies, teach them that one thing can be many things at once. Like a family of collective differences, but surrounded by a shared center.

Sometimes it's hard to relate to those we are related to. I find talking about food (and drinking wine) is a good place to start.

"What's your favorite kind of pasta?" you can ask.

Forgive them if they say "butter noodles."

CLAM CHOWDER DAY: 2/25

HOW DID BIVALVES GET TO BE ASSOCIATED WITH ROMANCE? OK, clams might be a stretch . . . but oysters as an aphrodisiac go all the way back in recorded history to Roman times. Roman sexy times. Orgy times. Ya dig?

Through my intensive online research I couldn't actually find anything to support the idea that the chemistry in an oyster makes you feel sexier, yet there's much documentation to support the fact that this belief was held by men in power. The infamous Casanova would eat up to fifty oysters at a time (GOOD GOD) before gallivanting off into the night. Napoleon ate oysters before battle. A little pocket of protein, the oyster is packed with nutrients and B vitamins, so it's fair to say that it gives you sustained energy and ability to execute. But does it make you horny? Chemically? No.

However, oysters and clams do remind people of vaginas, so I'm pretty sure that's why it made these dudes horny. Like how eating walnuts will make you smart because they look like brains. Ya know. Science.

The first time I had an oyster I was nine years old. We were out to dinner with a friend of the family, and he teasingly suggested I try an oyster from a passing sushi cart. The adults were all eating them, and I was a brilliant, tiny professor. So clearly, I had to show that I had the makings of greatness. And to do that I needed to do whatever the adults were doing. And at that moment, they were eating oysters.

My older sister had tried one and raved about its quality and texture. Delicious! she exclaimed. So unique. Unlike anything she'd had before in her thirteen years of life. As the conversation moved on, she leaned close to my ear and said, "Hannah, do NOT eat that."

Not to be outdone in maturity, I declared that I wanted an oyster too! There was one passing on a tiny Japanese boat rotating before us, and the man (our family friend, long story) placed it before me. Inviting me to try it and saying I would like it.

My sister kicked me from her side of the counter and widened her eyes to communicate in sibling "NO."

But who likes being told what to do?

I picked up the half shell and slurped it straight into my mouth. It moved faster than I thought and hit the back of my throat. I held back my gag and started to do what I thought I was supposed to do: I began chewing . . . and chewing . . .

"What are you doing? Don't chew it!"

The oyster was bursting in my mouth with salt and sea. Perhaps not the highest quality given our conveyer-belt sushi stop only had a B rating (if letter ratings existed in the 1990s).

"Hannah! Swallow!"

The battle waged within me. Humiliation. Defeat. Failure. Each pounded a beat in my chest. Money, money, money. The oysters were served on the black plate, which meant they were the most expensive. I had to swallow. I was wasting money. All these thoughts were racing through my mind as my mouth kept clenching around this textural nightmare. With one final desperate bid to swallow, I tilted my head back to force it down.

Unfortunately, there must have been a misfire in my mind because instead of hitting the "injest" button, my brain hit the "eject."

Perhaps it was the angle of my tilted head, perhaps it was the force of my convictions, but whatever the reason, this rejected oyster had tremendous force behind it. Shooting straight out of my mouth and arching down onto another passing sushi boat before us.

The restaurant was silent. I wanted to shrink into a tiny shell myself. The moment becoming a grain of sand in the muscles of my mind.

• • •

These days I love oysters! . . . Kind of.

I love the gesture that oysters provide. Love. Luxury. Expense. And if oysters don't appeal to you, make some clam chowder.

SEXY DATE-NIGHT OYSTERS

INGREDIENTS

Go to a restaurant and order oysters

1. Check the reviews. And health-inspector rating.

2. Bring a date you want to impress and suggest a light meal. Oysters, perhaps?

3. Don't bring the kids.

MARCH

UGH. MARCH.

In my humble opinion, this is the first month of the year that, frankly, sucks. It's such a weird, awkward, in-between kind of a month. Is it still winter? Is it spring? Why is it cold? Why am I hot? No one and nothing can seem to decide what kind of month March should be. There's no real holiday during it. I mean, I guess St. Patrick's Day, but if you don't live in New England, I can't imagine St. Paddy's means that much to you, and is being hungover in the middle of the workweek really that fun anymore?

OH! And March also has Mardi Gras! (Also sometimes in February.) Another drinking-heavy and culture-specific sort of celebration. But to be fair, what holiday isn't drinking-heavy and culture-specific?

March is the month when your New Year's resolutions are officially dead. The month after Valentine's, when you may or may not have ended or begun a new relationship. March is the awkward month of melting sleet and buds without blossoms. March is . . . well, frankly, a bit of a march in and of itself. With the fire of "new beginnings" dwindling down, what's there to keep you moving forward? What feeling is there to find aside from the sheer force of trudging along? Whoa . . . do I hate the month of March?!

Absolutely not.

The fact of the matter is that you're holding a book that believes there's always a special bit of something in everything. Sorry, St. Paddy! Sorry, Mardi Gras! We are here to celebrate something entirely different . . .

STARTING WITH . . .

KOSHER SALT
CELERY SALT
SMOKED SALT
ANT SALT
HIMALAYAN PINK SALT
BLACK HAWAIIAN SALT

GET OVER IT DAY: 3/9

AS I ENTER MY THIRTIES, I REALIZE HOW MANY BAD HABITS FROM MY TWENTIES I'VE CARRIED OVER. One of them being that when I screw something up, I have a really hard time letting go of that feeling of failure. Or when someone affronts me, I have a tendency to hold a grudge. And it's funny because I never think of myself as someone who holds a grudge.

I didn't even realize I was a grudge holder until recently. I always thought that "holding a grudge" implied some intention of vengeance. Retaliation. My response is so much more passive than that. I would call it more of a "fool me once, shame on *you*" mentality. More passive than active. The thought simply being *"Ah, you have betrayed me. I suppose now I'll have to . . . never trust you again."*

And that's clearly not super healthy. Yes, those relationships have been tested, and they've changed, but I realize I can turn the negative feelings into positive ones, into learning experiences. I can accept the circumstances and let the grudge dissolve.

Like salt in water.*

When salt dissolves in water, it bonds and forms something new. $NaCl + H_2O = NaClO + H_2$.

* Bet ya didn't think I was gonna find a way to relate this to salt. Well, joke is on you because I totally did—yeah, baby!

And that something new (salt water) is much more conductive than water alone. Electrically speaking. Salt water is quicker to react, quicker to transmit, and—if we apply this in the realm of human emotion—quicker to judge.

So when I've felt betrayed or had my trust broken, I become like salt water. I lose what was there before. And that's no good, is it? Because salt and water are great and powerful on their own . . . Separate is better.

A LIST OF MY FAVORITE SALTS

- TABLE SALT: THE MOST BASIC OF SALTS! A NECESSARY EVIL FOR SOME, A DANGEROUS DIETARY DESIRE FOR OTHERS. MY BELOVED AND HER FATHER BOTH ARE PRONE TO HYPERTENSION AND HIGH BLOOD PRESSURE. SO SALT LIGHTLY! (NOT PICTURED.)

- KOSHER SALT: I HAD TO LOOK UP WHAT THE DIFFERENCE WAS BETWEEN TABLE SALT AND KOSHER SALT. KOSHER SALT IS SALT THAT HASN'T BEEN IODIZED. ALSO BECAUSE OF THE SIZE OF THE CRYSTALS, IT DRAWS OUT MORE MOISTURE FROM THE MEAT. BLESSINGS OPTIONAL. MAZEL!

- CELERY SALT COMES FROM CELERY SEEDS. MOST COMMONLY USED TO FLAVOR SOUPS AND SUCH, IT CAN ALSO BE USED AS A KICK TO A SALAD OR A NICE ROAST.

- ANT SALT: THIS IS SALT MADE FROM ANTS. IT'S EXCELLENT. IT'S SPICY. IT'S ODDLY ZESTY. IT'S GREAT. ADD IT TO YOUR MEALS TO MAKE YOU APPEAR WELL-TRAVELED AND EXOTIC.

- BLACK HAWAIIAN SALT: THIS SALT IS LOADED WITH ACTIVATED CHARCOAL AND MINERALS FROM THE EARTH. EATING THIS SALT WILL MAKE YOU LIVE FOREVER! . . . OR AT LEAST THAT'S WHAT THE LATEST TRENDS WILL TELL YA. A LITTLE CHARCOAL ISN'T A

BAD THING, BUT IT CERTAINLY WON'T TURN BACK THE HANDS OF TIME.

- HIMALAYAN PINK SALT: THIS IS WHAT I LIKE TO THINK OF AS "VACATION SALT" BECAUSE EVERYONE ALWAYS COMES BACK FROM A VACATION WITH A TYPE OF PINK SALT. MAYBE THAT'S JUST ME, THOUGH . . . PERSONALLY I THINK OF SALT AS A GREAT GO-TO GIFT FOR ANY OCCASION.

- SMOKED SALT: I LOVE THE FLAVOR OF SOMETHING SMOKED . . . AND I LOVE SALT . . . BUT SMOKED SALT? NOT REALLY FOR ME. MAYBE I JUST DON'T KNOW HOW TO USE IT, BUT EVERY TIME I ADD IT TO SOMETHING IT OVERWHELMS THE FLAVORS. FRANKLY, I JUST LIKE TO TASTE IT RAW. NOT REALLY COOK WITH IT.

So, let's review. Salt is something that should help you enhance the flavors of a dish. Or it's something that you can use to cleanse. It's up to you which application of your "salt" you need to apply in your relationships.

In the end, just remember that if someone has hurt your feelings . . . don't be too salty.*

* For those reading who are post-millennial: SALTY (adj.), used to describe someone who is "angry, agitated, or upset," as well as someone who is "mean, annoying, and repulsive."

- CARROTS
- CABBAGE
- CUCUMBER
- JALAPEÑO
- CAULIFLOWER
- RADISH
- ONION
- ASPARAGUS
- GREEN BEANS
- STUFF YOU WANT IN A BLOODY MARY
- ANYTHING YOU FEEL COMFORTABLE PUTTING IN A JAR

BRINE BABIES

- RED WINE VINEGAR
- WHITE WINE VINEGAR
- RICE VINEGAR
- CIDER VINEGAR
- SALT
- SUGAR

PACK YOUR LUNCH DAY: 3/10

FLAVOR FRIENDS

SO MANY! THYME, DILL, ROSEMARY, OREGANO, MARJORAM, GARLIC CLOVES, GINGER, MUSTARD SEED, CORIANDER, PEPPERCORNS, RED PEPPER FLAKES, TURMERIC, OR SMOKED PAPRIKA!

HAPPY PACK YOUR LUNCH DAY! Ready to change your world one meal at a time?

• • •

I spend a lot of time on Reddit. My favorite subreddits include /r/whatisthisthing, /r/HumansBeingBros, and of course the ever-popular /r/oddlysatisfying. I go on this website to have a browsing experience that's not manufactured to my "taste." Meaning that I go on there and it shows me the internet in its purest form. A random sort of browsing not based on your Google search history, your e-mails, or your phone calls. Yes, I believe our phones are listening to us constantly, and frankly . . . I don't really care. Maybe if I get into politics one day I'll care. But until that day, I'll just keep loudly discussing my current wish lists and wait to see what shows up.

I like to go on Reddit because it also gives me a peek into the lives of others. The internet is so completely catered to our own tastes that "surfing the web" is really just hanging out inside our own echo chamber. And more often than not, when we hear about things that are happening outside of our own echo chamber, it's usually bad news. So, where do objectivity and discovery live? For me, that's on Reddit.

One of my personal favorite discoveries is a subreddit called /r/MealPrepSunday. It's basically a support forum for people who are preparing their lunches for the week ahead. It's a wonderful hub for people to support each other's goals, each and every one different from the other. Some people meal-prep to lose weight, others to save money, others to save time. No matter the goal behind the prepping, the group's support remains the same. People post pictures of their achievements, and others give praise in the form of upvotes and comments.

I myself don't meal-prep, but the subreddit did inspire me to try my hand at something I've never done before in the realm of preparation . . . or should I say preservation . . .

PICKLING: A BRIEF GLOBAL HISTORY

"PICKLING," IN SOME FORM OR ANOTHER, DATES ALL THE WAY BACK TO 2400 BC DURING THE ERA OF THE MESOPOTAMIANS. Fast-forward to 2030 BC and people started pickling cucumbers.* Fast-forward again to 50 BC and we find ourselves in ancient Egypt, where Cleopatra is attributing her beauty to the benefits of eating pickles daily. I also attribute the beauty of my beloved Ella to her constant consumption of pickles.

My personal pickle history began with sauerkraut—a great big jar of cabbage ready to accompany any meal. That counts as eating vegetables, right?

After that, the pickling of radishes found in many Asian cuisines completely fascinated me. How is this vegetable—which I would never normally eat—so crunchy and cool and crisp when pickled? Pickling is a wondrous art. And here's how you can join the annals of history and do it yourself.

P.S. IF YOU'RE HOPING TO MAKE LONGER-LASTING PRESERVES . . . THEN READ ANOTHER COOKBOOK BECAUSE I DON'T WANT TO LEAD YOU ASTRAY. THE BABIES LISTED ON THE PREVIOUS PAGES SHOULD LAST YOU MAYYYYBE A MONTH. BUT I WOULDN'T RISK IT. JUST DO IT FOR A PARTY SO YOU CAN FEEL COOL.

* Which are native to India! Did you know that? Wild. This book is full of learning!

BASICS OF PICKLING

- LEARN A LITTLE BIT ABOUT PICKLING BY READING THIS BOOK! PRETTY COOL, RIGHT? YOU'RE LEARNING AND LAUGHING! (HOPEFULLY.)

- PREP YOUR VEGGIES. CUT THIN SLICES, CUT LITTLE CIRCLES, CUT THEM TO THE SIZE OF THE JAR OR UNDER. THAT'S ALL YOU NEED TO KNOW TO PREP YOUR VEGGIES. SO APPROACHABLE!

- IF YOU'RE TRYING TO PICKLE SOMETHING LIKE GREEN BEANS OR ASPARAGUS AND YOU WANNA MAINTAIN A CRUNCHY-CRUNCHY, THEN GIVE THEM A QUICK BLANCHING (HOT WATER, THEN COLD) BEFORE PUTTING THEM IN THE JAR.

- MAKE YOUR BRINE. ALL THIS MEANS IS MIXING THE TYPE OF VINEGAR YOU WANT WITH WATER AND PUTTING IT IN A POT. HOW DO YOU FIGURE OUT WHAT KIND OF VINEGAR YOU WANNA USE? GIVE THEM A SNIFF! GIVE THEM A TASTE! THINK ABOUT THE THING YOU'RE TRYING TO PICKLE. DOES IT LEAN SWEET LIKE A CARROT? USE A CIDER VINEGAR! IS IT BLAND LIKE A RADISH? GIVE CIDER VINEGAR A SHOT HERE TOO!

- ADD YOUR SUGAR AND YOUR SALT (THIS IS ALL TO TASTE), AND BRING YOUR BRINE TO A BOIL SO ALL OF THE CRYSTALS HAVE DISSOLVED.

- OH, DID I MENTION TO PUT ALL YOUR HERBS AND YOUR VEGGIES IN A JAR? DO THAT.

- NOW! POUR YOUR BEAUTIFUL BRINE OVER YOUR VEGGIES AND MARVEL AT YOUR OWN INGENUITY. WOW. I SURE HOPE THIS DOESN'T POISON ANYBODY.

- REMOVE AIR BUBBLES BY GIVING YOUR JAR KISSES!! OR TAPPING THE SIDES.

- SEAL AND REFRIGERATE! IN A COUPLE DAYS THESE SHOULD BE GOOD TO GO!

RAVIOLI DAY: 3/20

WORKING ON A RELATIONSHIP WITH YOURSELF IS NO EASY TASK, BUT THE END RESULTS ARE DEEPLY REWARDING. It's a laborious process that can involve developing new tools *and then* properly using those tools with your newfound skills. And how do we develop these skills? Practice.

Consider the ravioli, a palate-pleasing pocket of potential. What's inside the ravioli can change, but the shape to get there and contain it remains the same. The making of ravioli from scratch requires many different tools and a moderate amount of patience. Of course, in the beginning of this process, you'll need to acquire the tools necessary, from there you will probably make a failed batch that slowly begins to resemble ravioli, and then eventually you'll be able to whip up a batch of ravioli with ease. Maybe even . . . enjoyment?

The skills necessary for making ravioli remind me of the skills that I've had to learn in couples therapy. I'm engaged, and having witnessed

multiple divorces in my family and among my peers, I plan on doing everything in my power to set this partnership up for success. Once I had a therapist tell me that people don't just have affairs. That affairs are symptoms of dysfunction within a relationship. And if you can avoid dysfunction, then you can avoid affairs. Maybe. Theoretically? Who's to say! Look, you're taking advice from a "cookbook" that's barely about "cooking" so . . . just admire how pretty that ravioli picture is! Beautiful!

RAVIOLI A LA (CONFLICT) RESOLUTION

INGREDIENTS

Flour

Water

Salt

Eggs

Olive oil

1. Combine your flour and salt. *Take turns listening to each other's experience without comment.*

2. Make a well in your flour and add eggs. *Make room in your emotional experience to see it from their perspective.*

3. Mix that all together by hand. *Say things like "I can see why you'd feel that way." Show compassion for their experience.*

4. Add olive oil and knead. *Stay connected with your body. If you feel it tensing, take a deep breath and stay focused on the conversation at hand.*

5. Set aside for 30 minutes to let your dough rise. *If you're getting too hot under the collar, take a 10-minute break and reset. Write down what it is you want them to hear. What is your goal for the conversation? What do you want them to know?*

6. Roll your dough out to very thin and cut it into small circles or squares. *Make a plan for next time an issue like this comes up.*

7. Stuff, boil, eat. *Kiss and make up.*

Some people are born with "pasta makers" (stability and support) and "rolling cutters" (access and ability). Some of us aren't and have to learn how to do everything "from scratch." Just because your attempts at ravioli might not turn out like those of people with all the necessary tools from the get-go doesn't mean they won't be just as tasty. After all, it's what's on the inside that counts.

I AM IN CONTROL DAY: 3/30

EGGS ARE TRANSFORMATIVE OBJECTS. They can take on a wide array of shapes and styles (boiled, coddled, poached, fried, scrambled, flat, basted, shirred, custard'd, tea'd, omelette'd . . . yes, these last ones aren't real words, but you get what I'm saying . . . the list goes on!) and contribute to a wide variety of cooking and baking. Eggs are magic!

Which is why it shouldn't be too surprising to learn that many cultures do believe eggs are, in fact . . . magic. The sort of magic that could give you the fleeting feeling of control in your life.

NATURAL
CAGE FREE
LARGE EGGS

DISCLAIMER: As an insufferable white lady, I have no idea what I'm talking about. However, there are many people who do! Don't mess with energies without guidance. Burn some protective incense, dab on some essential oils, make sure you've cleansed your environment before messing around with any of this stuff. You don't want to invite anything in that you don't want there. And I don't want you guys coming back to haunt me! I'm just saying it's something to look into, and here's a little taste of how to do it.

• • •

Here is one of my favorite beliefs about the mystical quality of eggs, as inspired by a Mexican tradition I've been fortunate enough to witness:

EGG BLESSINGS

INGREDIENTS

Eggs

Water

White candle

Some sort of spiritual belief system and a willingness to let go

1. Take some deep breaths. Center yourself. Chill out . . . and maybe close the windows, because do you really want anyone seeing what you're about to do?

2. Play some groovy tunes that make you feel positive and light. Light the candle and set your intention of what you're hoping this egg will absorb from your bod.*

3. Rub that egg on your bod! Start at your crown and work your way down. Take extra time at your temples, because if those eggs are cold, it will feel amazing and like you're at a little egg-based spa. Under your eyes and

across your sinuses too. It feels great. Go over your arms, take your time over your chest and heart, keep going, and then . . . you're done! And nobody saw! Woo-hoo!

4. In this Mexican tradition of egg cleansing, you then break the egg into a glass of water. You can read it and look for signs of what was pulled from your body. Then dump the whole thing into the toilet and flush it all away. Bye-bye, bad juju!

* EXAMPLE: I FEEL CLUTTERED AND OVERWHELMED SOMETIMES. I DESCRIBE THIS FEELING AS THERE NOT BEING ENOUGH SPACE BETWEEN MY MOLECULES. SO, SOMETHING I WOULD THINK OF IS . . . REMOVING ANYTHING I DON'T NEED. THE THINGS I DON'T NEED TO CARRY. NEGATIVE ENERGY THAT'S LINGERED A LITTLE TOO LONG. A MEAN INTERACTION WITH A STRANGER. ANTICIPATORY ANXIETY ABOUT EVENTS MONTHS IN THE FUTURE. FEAR FOR A FRIENDSHIP THAT'S ALREADY PROVEN ITSELF. THAT SORT OF THING.

AP-
RIL

SPRING HAS SPRUNG, MOTHERFUCKER!

Let the flower crowns begin! Who's ready for festival season?!

. . . Me neither.

April may not have an obvious "Ap-thrill," but there's a lot of celebration to be had in this dandy little time of year. For instance, I consider April to be the month of disbelief! Take note of how many people around you say "I can't believe it's April already!" and you'll see what I mean.

April is also a magical month in terms of its holidays. This is the month where we celebrate our foolish foibles and other vague mysteries of life. For instance, did you know that there is a magical bunny that brings eggs? And that bunny loves Jesus! Amazing!

In this month we'll also be celebrating the beauty of our planet and its dwindling habitability. After celebrating Earth Day this year, you may end up feeling more scared . . . but also more prepared.

LET'S BEGIN!

APRIL FOOLS' DAY: 4/1

I'M AN IDIOT.

Now this may come as no surprise to you, but it still comes as a surprise to me. I've always thought I was resourceful, but maybe it's just desperate. A prime example being this morning, talking to my partner about my deadline for writing and saying, "Apparently, the publisher is worried. I had no idea we were in bad shape! I didn't know that."

To which she replied: "How could you not?"

To which I realized: *I'm an idiot.*

There are many things that make someone an idiot (I think). And for me (I think) it must come from having a burned-out amygdala (maybe). Put simply, the amygdala is the part of your brain that contributes to emotional response. Specifically to threat, fear, emergency. It controls that panic in your body that fires off letting you know that something is in jeopardy. This adorable almond-shaped bit of brain matter dictates how you process urgency. Mine is slow on the uptake. Which makes me a very calm person in crisis. And a person who is very slow to pick up on things that I don't perceive as actual danger. Like book deadlines.

(However, it does like to fire off panic in environments that, in its weird backward-idiot logic, it perceives as threats. Like shopping malls. But who doesn't hate aimlessly walking around a shopping mall, amirite? Go in, get item, get out. That's the way, *uh-huh uh-huh,* I like it.)

So! It takes a lot to make me feel like we are in jeopardy unless there is physical jeopardy. It takes a lot to make me feel like something is at stake when the stakes are arbitrary. I don't pick up on it until someone is like, "How can you not?" Then I realize, *Oh. Everyone is scared. I should be scared too.*

If you think of your flaws and foolishness as something positive, you can find the way in your life that it benefits you. For me, embracing my foolishness has led me to a world of improvisation and meal making that I'd never thought I'd enter, let alone enjoy.

So I may be a bit of an idiot. But I think I'm okay with that. It's given me a lot of wonderful memories . . .

TEN MY DRUNK KITCHEN FOIBLES

1. THIS IS A CLASSIC: REPLACING SUGAR WITH SALT AND ABSOLUTELY DESTROYING A BATCH OF BAKED GOODS. IN MY CASE, IT WAS SCONES. SUCH A BUMMER. I LOVE GETTING SCONED!

2. I'VE NEVER SUCCESSFULLY MADE A MERINGUE. HAVE YOU? IT'S IMPOSSIBLE. I BELIEVE IT'S VOODOO OR WITCHCRAFT OR SOMETHING SIMILAR. WHOEVER BELIEVES THAT YOU'LL KNOW WHEN YOU'VE SUCCESSFULLY CREATED SOFT PEAKS HAS CLEARLY NEVER EXPANDED THEIR DEFINITION OF "PEAKS" TO INCLUDE . . . WELL, FRANKLY ANYTHING THAT'S NOT A SMOOTH SURFACE. HOW SOFT IS SOFT? I'M GETTING ALL WORKED UP JUST THINKING ABOUT HOW IMPOSSIBLE MERINGUE IS. AND FRANKLY, I DON'T EVEN LIKE THE WAY IT TASTES. IT TASTES LIKE AN EXCUSE. WELCOME IN THE MOMENT, BUT ULTIMATELY SUBSTANCELESS.

3. ONE TIME I WAS ATTEMPTING HOMEMADE PRINGLES, AND I WAS USING A WINEGLASS LIKE A COOKIE CUTTER AND ACCIDENTALLY BROKE IT INTO THE BATTER I WAS WORKING WITH.

4. ONE TIME I MADE A GELATIN-LIKE PIE AND JUST . . . DROPPED THE WHOLE THING ON THE FLOOR.

5. MANY TIMES I'VE BURNED MANY THINGS. INCLUDING M'SELF.

6. ONE TIME I TRIED TO MAKE A CROISSANT AND WAS SO UTTERLY BROKEN BY THE IMPOSSIBLE TASK OF MAINTAINING THE TEMPERATURE OF THE BUTTER WHILE ROLLING AND FOLDING THE DOUGH (YOU HAVE TO PUT IT IN THE FRIDGE, AND TAKE IT OUT, AND PUT IT IN, AND TAKE IT OUT) THAT I VOWED NEVER TO BAKE AGAIN.

7. ONE TIME I TRIED TO MAKE A DELICIOUS PASTA WITH A WHITEFISH I HAD NEVER USED BEFORE . . . AND INSTEAD OF BUYING IT SEASONED, I ACCIDENTALLY BOUGHT IT . . . PICKLED.

8. I'VE BEEN OVERLY KNEADY.

9. THERE WAS A PERIOD OF TIME WHEN MY BLENDER HAD A PERSONAL VENDETTA AGAINST ME. NO MATTER HOW MANY TIMES SOMEONE SHOWED ME HOW TO PUT IT ON AND TAKE IT OFF, I COULDN'T GET THE HANG OF IT. WHAT WAS THE CAUSE? PROBABLY MISCHIEVOUS KITCHEN FAIRIES.

10. ONE TIME I WAS MAKING A FILLING FOR A PIE AND ACCIDENTALLY MADE A DELICIOUS JAM INSTEAD. I DON'T CONSIDER THAT A MISTAKE. I JUST NEEDED TO REFRAME MY INTENTION ON THAT ONE.

This year for April Fools' Day, I invite you to embrace the part of yourself that feels like an idiot. Maybe there's something that you're not good at, and no matter how hard you try, you just can't change it. So stop trying to change it. Embrace it. Will you make mistakes? Absolutely.

But on the other side of making that mistake, there's a lesson to be learned, a memory to be made, and some unexpected company along the way. (Except for the bit about salt and sugar. Just label those. It's a real pain to make that mistake more than once.)

ARE YOU TIRED? Do you feel your eyes getting droopy as you read this book? Is that afternoon cup of coffee just not working the way it used to, only kicking in at 8 or 9 p.m., when you finally have time to rest but find yourself over-whelmingly awake, needing to take a walk around the block just to calm down and get out of your head? Word.

The thing about your body's energy is that it might not be just about "caffeine." And not all types of "caffeine" respond the same way inside our bodies. And sometimes it might not be about caffeine at all!

So here are some facts about sleepiness that might be worth examining this Walking Day while you're pacing around your neighborhood.

WALKING DAY:

FIRST WEDNESDAY OF THE MONTH

Vitamin Deficiency

Our body works like a mosaic. Many different nutrients and elements comprise the whole. Some of these elements we call vitamins. If you find yourself prone to a constant and perpetual sleepiness, ask your doctor to check your hormones and vitamin D levels. If your doctor says, “Well, you might just need to exercise more,” then reply by saying, “Tell ya what, you do these blood tests and then we’ll talk.” Due to our indoors-only lifestyles, a whopping 42 percent of Americans are vitamin D deficient. You could be one of them! If you are, your blood will show it, and if it’s significant your doctor can give you a prescription for something that will actually work. (Note that not all drugstore vitamins are effective. There’s no regulation on vitamins. So some of the brands are just BS.)

Hydration

Say it with me . . . drink more water! But what if you drink water all day and still feel chronically thirsty? Well, maybe you need salt. Or electrolytes. Experiment with what quenches you. If you listen, your body will tell you what you need.

Deeper Sleep

Lolololololololol, as an insomniac, lemme tell you that sleep doesn’t dictate my energy level at all. Sometimes when I get eight hours of sleep, I feel *exhausted* the next day. Last night, I fell asleep at 3:30 and woke up at 7. And today I feel amazing! Will I take a nap later? You betcha!

And last but not least . . .

ZZZ

Caffeine

Caffeine keeps you awake by stressing your body out. Chronic coffee drinkers experience high levels of cortisol (fun fact, cortisol makes a playful ring of fat around your stomach, so even people with the healthiest meals might not be losing the weight "where they want to" because of the body's stress response to coffee and the storage of fat). Sometimes the best way to wake up when you're feeling sleepy is to go for a walk. If people can take a "smoke break" or get up to "get a cup of coffee" then you also have every right to get up and leave your desk to take a freakin' walk. People aren't made to be trapped indoors all day, every day, all year, every year. So be the master of your universe. Get up and take a walk if you feel like it. And if anybody stops you, just look at them and say:

"I'm celebrating Walking Day!"

. . . And then hurry off before they have a chance to Google it. Speedy speedy!

LOVE OUR CHILDREN DAY:

PROBABLY THE FIRST SATURDAY OF THE MONTH (AND EASTER TOO, KIND OF)

HAPPY EASTER, EVERYBODY!

But since I don't celebrate Easter, we're gonna celebrate Love Our Children Day instead. Here is a fun crafting activity that you can do this Easter to celebrate another day of being alive on the planet. Hey, let's make a guy who apparently was alive TWICE.

HOW TO MAKE A JESUS EGG

INGREDIENTS

Egg

Sharpie

Hot glue gun

Or superglue

Or any glue

Napkins from somewhere like a café or something. If you can only find white napkins, then make a bunny or Santa instead!

A group of children or playful adults

FUN FACT: EASTER IS A REALLY SWEET HOLIDAY TO CELEBRATE WITH YOUR KIDS. IF THERE'S A WAY YOU CAN MAKE IT WORK FOR YOUR FAMILY, THEN THAT'S AWESOME. I THINK GOING ON AN "EGG HUNT" AND SPENDING THE DAY CRAFTING TOGETHER IS ALL YOUR KIDS REALLY WANT. SLOW DOWN. LOVE YOUR CHILDREN. PLAY WITH THEM. ONE DAY THEY'LL BE GROWN AND YOU'LL MISS THE MAGIC YOU MUTUALLY MADE.

1. Decide whether you want to eat this egg later or if you want to keep it. If you want to eat it, then hard-boil it (and maybe ask yourself why you want to eat Jesus. Oh, wait! People totally do that! Did I just invent Catholicism?!).

2. If you don't want to eat the egg later and DO want to keep the egg, then poke a tiny hole in Jesus's butt and . . . ya know what, I'm just gonna stop right there. You get it.

3. Rip up tiny pieces of the paper napkin for the hair and beard.

4. Ask the kids you're with if they still believe in Santa.

5. Tell everybody in the room that Jesus was actually a pretty cool guy and super liberal. And never said anything bad about gay people. Or any people! Except people who take money in the church.* Does your church take your money? Wow! Bet Jesus would have hated that.

6. Ask if you can stay even though you've insulted someone's religious beliefs.

7. Glue on the hair and draw a tiny face.

8. Say, "Awww," because it's pretty dang cute, isn't it?

9. #JesusEgg

* Temple, technically, or tabernacle.

L QILLA
BASMATI RICE
MALAI
G OF RICE
Imports, Inc.
BEEF
CHILI
14 oz
MASTER
SPORTSMAN
NINA
ITALIAN PEELED
PEELED TOMATOES
GOYA
PRODUCT OF INDIA
GOYAL BASMATI RICE

EARTH DAY: 4/22

I OFTEN OVERHEAR PEOPLE DISCUSSING HOW IMPORTANT IT IS FOR US TO "SAVE THE PLANET" OR BRINGING UP ALL THE EVIDENCE THAT SHOWS "THE PLANET IS DYING." It takes a lot of willpower to keep from pointing out what seems obvious to me: The planet isn't dying—the planet doesn't need saving . . . The humans on the planet have fucked themselves, and now the earth is kicking them out.

So, the planet is gonna be just fine. It's a big rock existing in the vacuum of space. Surrounded by an innumerable amount of other big rocks and gas giants of varying sizes colliding and orbiting each other for eons past and eons forward. (In fact, these majesties have existed so long that the concept of eons actually belittles their age.)

Our adorable home rock has been circling in existence for about 4.5 billion years. The dominant species of *Homo sapiens* (that's us—last surviving member of the *Homo* genus) has been the apex predator for a measly seventy thousand years. In that time we have done a phenomenal job of shooting ourselves in the foot (in some cases quite literally) and rendering our planet uninhabitable. Or soon to be.

Let's break this down even further: Our current style of modern living has had many negative effects on the planet around us. The planet, in its wisdom and natural response to these effects, is following suit. Like a body fighting off a parasite, the earth is rejecting us. We used to maintain a symbiotic relationship back when we were smaller and patient and learning how to grow and farm and find abundance. Unfortunately, abundance is subjective, and every generation or so decides that they want more—more product, more speed, more years, more babies, and so on. Now we find ourselves dazed and confused, as our planet has looked at our requests and decided the only solution is for there to be less. Less what? Less people. Less habitable environments. Less.

So, no. The planet isn't dying. It doesn't need to be saved. We pose no actual threat to it.

Our greatest threat is to ourselves.

• • •

Recently, my older sister has become pretty obsessed with doomsday prepping. She and her neuroscientist husband have devoted the majority of their household and partnership to discussing and planning for the most likely version of doom to befall us. The likely threat is ever-changing, and I've been fortunate enough to hear survival strategies for a number of scenarios. Currently, they believe that a group of the super-rich is going to eliminate the more impoverished population through a super-virus and genetic attack. They give us all about a year. Which is honestly a relief to me because I've got the rest of this book to write and I have been feeling stressed.

Biochemical warfare and the evil of the ultrarich aside, doomsday preppers have a lot to fear. And to be fair, some of the arguments have a good amount of reason behind them. Bless the internet! There's a lot of evidence to help feed that fear. (Did you know 98 percent of the bugs in Puerto Rico are gone? That's what I heard! My God!)

I'm not here to debate whether the world is going to end. We know for a fact that the world will end. But for now my world is alive and well, so I've decided the best I can do is prepare myself to maintain that world for as long as possible.

Doomsday Prep

You're going to want a big bag of basic grains.

But you need water to make grains happen.

Okay, good point, so you're going to want as much water as you can store within reason in your home.

But doesn't that keep you kind of landlocked to your apartment or room or house or whatever? What about other people trying to fight you for resources?

Okay, that's a good point, it's probably better to be mobile because you don't know if your environment will remain stable (not to mention the greatest threat—other people).

Okay! So you're going to want some sort of portable water-making thing.

What?

I don't know, like something that can pull water out from the air, hopefully? Condensation? Look, I'm basing this mostly off the one moment of *Waterworld* that I remember, when Kevin Costner is floating at sea and he pees into a tube and water comes out. Does that exist yet? I have an eager bladder, so I am good to go.

I don't think that's real.

Well, fuck, idk.

I live in the city of Los Angeles, in the state of California, in the (currently) United States of America, on the continent of North America, off the coast of the Pacific Ocean, which is on the "Ring of Fire," so the number one thing I should be preparing for is . . . earthquakes.

See? Reason can be applied!

Now, in my city, there are areas that are prone to other types of doom (flooding, fire, etc.), but where I live the number one concern that could take us by surprise would be an earthquake. Fires don't apply to me. But they might still apply to you, so research thusly!

I grew up in California, so earthquakes are nothing new to me. I was three years old during the 1989 earthquake that collapsed freeways and left 1.4 million people without power.

California is also very prone to droughts, but given our previous water-making conundrum, I've chosen to focus on earthquakes for the purpose of this example of reasonable preparedness.

Once this imaginary earthquake happens, society won't all collapse at once. It will dissolve before it collapses. Whisper, not a bang. So it's not like I need to suddenly prepare to hit the road and go rogue. I've watched doomsday-prepper shows, and I see those guys driving around in their trucks-turned-tanks (or tanks-turned-trucks) and discussing how they are going to protect themselves from the desperate and clawing masses they think will suddenly descend upon them. Meanwhile, I think to myself, *How the hell are they going to get gas to power those things? Why are they doing this? Are they doing this because of the fear that other people are going to do it first? Isn't that a self-fulfilling prophecy? Why am I watching this show? . . . Yes, we should watch the next episode.*

I've also realized that it's important to think of these things in terms of surviving one stage at a time. For example, a catastrophic earthquake in LA will not leave the rest of the nation without resources. In an ideal world we have a government that sends people federal aid when they are struggling. However, in order to get to that point, it's probably best to pick a set number of days one could survive without anyone's aid at all.

It's also important to pick the amount of space you're going to dedicate to your preparation. (I feel like the space dictates it more than anything else. For instance, I live in a two-bedroom apartment, so the amount of doomsday storage we have is minimal. We are looking at a three- to five-day prep. *C'est la vie!* Sounds good! A reasonable start point is all we need.)

I would say out of all the things to be afraid of—the many valid things to fear—my greatest fear is that I will feel so overwhelmed by the constant onslaught of information and bad things that are happening that I will lose sight of the things that could happen to me. The overwhelming logic of "I can't prepare for it ALL, so should I prepare in even the slightest way for ANYTHING?"

My answer is yes. So take a deep breath, step back, and think it through. Not too much, just a little. Just do what you can when you can, and trust that whatever you can do will be enough. Something is always more than nothing.

Also, I just don't have anywhere to park a tank. It's LA, people. Traffic sucks.

MAY

MAY IS THE FIFTH MONTH OF OUR TWELVE MONTHS OF CELEBRATION! MAY IS A FISTFUL OF FESTIVITIES! FIVE FINGERS FULL OF FUN!

For the month of May we are going to be celebrating a spring of self-renewal. Summer is just around the corner, and some of us may already be feeling the burn.

Will you be graduating this May? GOOD LUCK AND GOD BLESS.

Will you be a mother for the first time this Mother's Day? GOOD LUCK AND GOD BLESS.

Will you be looking for a spring fling to chase away the last vestiges of those lonely winter nights? GOOD LUCK AND GOD BLESS.

The month of May gives us a chance to do a bit of self-check-in to make sure we aren't going to go "self-wreck-in" all summer long. "Bikini season" is a term you'll be hearing this month. Just start ignoring that now. One-pieces are pretty hot. At least in my humble opinion. Less is more! Less showing of skin = more wonders within . . .

And that's exactly what this month is going to be about for us as we celebrate doing less and getting more. We are going to be celebrating self-care, self-indulgence, and so much more!

Well, not *too* much more. Like just two more things. Hey, look, we aren't even halfway through the year yet. It's a marathon—not a sprint.

Oh! And I'd also like to celebrate flowers. I really love flowers. Remember the skunk from *Bambi*? That's me. Except add congested sinuses and seasonal allergies.

SO. WITHOUT FURTHER ACHOO . . .

» (ME) LOYALTY DAY: 5/1 «

LOYALTY DAY IS A DAY SET ASIDE TO REAFFIRM LOYALTY TO THE UNITED STATES. Really.

It's also May Day. Which is also the first day of summer.

Loyalty Day is about showing loyalty to your country. May Day is about splendors of spring. So what if we combined the two and made it into something new:

"Me Loyalty Day"!

This year show yourself some love by giving your face a much-needed vacation. Can you believe what we put our skin through on the regular? Sunshine, pollutants, slobbery kisses from the neighbor's dog-beast. The works! Our faces go with us everywhere and do everything. But what do we do for our faces? Aside from occasional wash and moisturize, they go pretty much neglected. So that's why this Me Loyalty Day you're going to be pledging to the one that really never lets you down!*

With a food-based facial!

* Until it starts sagging, that is. I can picture exactly what kind of old person I am gonna look like. Forget family jewels . . . it's gonna be family jowls!

FOR YOUR FACE

INGREDIENTS
FACE-SAFE FOODS:

Avocado

Honey

Yogurt

Other possibilities include strawberry, lemon, baking soda (as a cleanser), oatmeal, banana, coconut, oat, and olive oil

1. Start out with some affirmations! Ooh, or maybe discover a sassy new catchphrase that you'll say to people whether that response is warranted or not: "It's me time, baby!"

2. Before doing anything to anything, you'll want to clean off your sur-face. You wouldn't cook in a dirty pan, would you? No! Of course not! So get that dirty pan you call a face to the closest sink and give it a solid cleanse.

3. Get out your ingredients. For my mask I used only yogurt, honey, and avocado because I have dry skin. But you can find more possibilities in the list at left or on the internet. Have fun with it!

4. Mix everything together! I would do a ratio of like 3-2-1, avocado-yogurt-honey. Oh! And be sure to get a full-fat yogurt. As pure as you can find it. I want something that's as fresh as the grassland animal from which it came!

5. Rub this all over your face. It's okay if some gets in your mouth, but not your eyes. You can use this wait time as an opportunity to slice up some cold cucumber and put it in a glass of water—spa day!—and do that whole thing. But I always feel like it's wasting a good cuke . . . said the girl who took a precious avocado and mashed it onto her face . . . hm . . . Maybe I need to rethink a few things.

6. Wait fifteen minutes. Deep breaths. Meditate. This is your me time, dammit! The point is don't rush it. Unless you're having an allergic reaction. Then rush yourself to the ER!

7. Wash off your mug and take a look at the beauty before you. Refreshed anew!

There are lots of face-safe foods, btw. Mix and match to your heart's content. Find the facial profile that's right for you. Do what feels right for you. But definitely don't experiment too much because it is . . . after all . . . your face. O_O

NOTE: DON'T EXFOLIATE EVERY DAY. THAT WILL HURT YOUR SWEET BABY SKIN. ONCE—MAYYYYBE TWICE—A WEEK IS BEST. AND BE GENTLE! ALSO FACTOR IN HORMONES. MY SKIN IS CLEAR TWENTY DAYS OUT OF THE MONTH, BUT FOR THE REMAINING TEN, I ALWAYS GET A HANDFUL OF LARGE, PAINFUL, HORMONAL ZITS THAT LET ME KNOW MY EMOTIONS ARE ABOUT TO GO TOTALLY HAYWIRE. AH, THE JOYS OF BEING ALIVE!

O_O

EAT WHAT YOU WANT DAY: 5/11

YOU KNOW HOW SOMETIMES YOU'RE LOOKING FORWARD TO YOUR SPECIAL TREAT YOU'VE BEEN SAVING—LIKE THE LAST DARK-CHOCOLATE HÄAGEN-DAZS BAR IN THE FREEZER . . . OR THE LEFTOVERS FROM A LUNCH YOU SAVED FOR DINNER—BUT THEN YOU'VE COME HOME AND SOMEONE HAS EATEN IT? Doesn't that suck? . . .

It's important for you to maintain your identity and individuality at all times, especially when it comes to saving your special treats. Otherwise, if you're like me, you end up just giving everything away because sharing feels good. But after the good feeling you get from sharing has passed, you might not have anything left that you've saved for yourself.

So if you're looking forward to something, tell people that it's yours, and it's special, and you're looking forward to it. You'd be amazed at how much people can respect that.

. . . Or you can just hide it.

SECRET STASH

- GO RUN ALL THE ERRANDS AND DO ALL THE CHORES BECAUSE SOMEHOW IT'S BEEN DECIDED THAT YOU'RE THE PERSON WHO MAINTAINS THE HOUSEHOLD. EVEN AFTER YOU SET UP THAT HELPFUL CHORE WHEEL AND ASSIGNED PEOPLE DESIGNATED TASKS.*

- WHILE GROCERY SHOPPING, SPY A LITTLE SOMETHING THAT CATCHES YOUR EYE. OOH. MAMA LIKEY.

- REALIZE THAT IF YOU COME HOME WITH THIS, THEN EVERYONE WILL POUNCE ON IT AT ONCE. WHAT ARE YOU TO DO?

- HIDE IT.

- NO. YOU CAN'T . . .

- . . . OR CAN YOU?

- JUST DO IT. EVERYONE HAS SECRETS, RIGHT? MAYBE YOU CAN HAVE A LITTLE SECRET TOO. A SPECIAL SPACE THAT'S JUST FOR YOU. IT'S NOT LIKE YOU'RE HURTING ANYBODY . . . WHAT THEY DON'T KNOW WON'T HURT THEM. AND FRANKLY, LAST TIME YOU CAME HOME WITH A TREAT, IT WAS GONE BEFORE YOU GOT A CHANCE TO SAVOR IT. YOU'RE THE SLOWEST EATER IN THE HOUSE, BUT THAT'S JUST BECAUSE YOU LIKE TO TAKE YOUR TIME, DAMMIT! DON'T LET THOSE HEATHENS TAKE THIS AWAY FROM YOU!

- YOU DO LOVE THOSE HEATHENS, THOUGH. WE KNOW THAT.

- BUT YOU LOVE YOURSELF TOO.

* It should be noted, though, that maybe people could have a chance to get it done if you didn't just jump in and do it yourself. But doing it right away is better than waiting, right? Maybe. Maybe not.

This is all to say that it's okay to designate spaces for yourself. Just like time in the bathtub, time at the gym, or time when everyone else is out of the house and you've got the place *all to yourself*. Whatever your secret stash may be (material or otherwise), take today to celebrate the space you've made for everyone. Including you.

VIKING
INDIA
MEXICO
THE COOKBOOK
MOMOFUKU

MOTHER'S DAY:

SECOND SUNDAY OF THE MONTH

ALL OF MY FRIENDS' CHILDREN ARE AROUND THE SAME AGE RIGHT NOW. Eighteen to twenty-four months. Which in baby terms means they are entering into toddlerdom but with varying stages of verbal ability. As a friend without children, I think this is honestly the best time to spend with them. Once they reach the age of being an actual *kid*, things get wayyyyy more complicated. Babies are always learning; they are never bored. They may get distracted, they may want to move from object to object, they may want you to bounce a tiny ball with them or stuff a bunch of tissue paper into a box and pull it all back out . . . only to stuff it all back in again. The point is that babies may require a lot of attention, but at least their attention isn't difficult to hold.

Unlike kids. Kids get "bored."

And for adults, kids . . . can get boring.

My favorite way to interact with all lesser beings—I MEAN PRECIOUS YOUTHS—is to treat them like adults and give them adult tasks and jobs. When my little sister was eight years old, we used to play a game called "Restaurant" where she would pretend to be a waiter in a high-end establishment and have to meet my haughty, elitist demands.

A more simplified version of this is to take your children and teach them what it means to work in a kitchen. Starting with the fun part . . . the food.

TINY CHEF COMPETITION

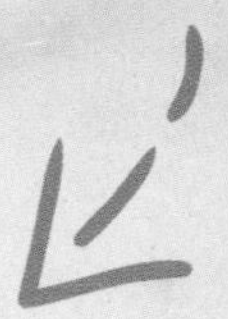

INGREDIENTS

Plain spaghetti

Fruits

Avocados

Cheerios

And enough spices and seasonings to make them feel like they are actually doing something inventive and creative

Buy yourself a whistle, a clipboard, and a stopwatch. You're committed.

And some rosé

1. Figure out if you're more of a referee or a coach. In the beginning you might have to be a coach and show them the ropes, but from there you can start to pit them against each other to build a healthy sense of sportsmanship.

2. Set out all the ingredients, and remind them that whatever they use they will have to help clean. This is like the idea of "single-pan cooking" and will help them process cause and effect. Damn, you're a great parent.

3. Tell them it's okay to taste as they go! (I assume you know what allergies your babies have . . . If not . . . maybe figure that out first.)

4. Be prepared to taste whatever they've made . . . So maybe have a glass of wine beforehand.

5. Really emphasize how delicious it is and declare that everyone who participated is a winner. If they complain about that (or some passing adult gives you shit for saying that everyone's a winner), then say this:

"WELL, I GUESS THE REAL WINNER IS THE ONE WHO HAD THE MOST FUN."

FUN FACT: THE GLASSES IN THIS PHOTO ARE MY FAVORITE GLASSES. OR RATHER . . . THEY WERE. UNTIL I LOST THEM. I AM SO SAD, BUT SO HAPPY THAT THEY ARE FOREVER IMMORTALIZED IN THIS BOOK. RIP HUDSON IN GOLD!

BE A MILLIONAIRE DAY: 5/20

THEY SAY MONEY CAN'T BUY HAPPINESS . . . BUT IT CAN BUY THERAPY! Which is why I believe all people who make above six figures should be required by law to go to therapy. And if you make above SEVEN figures, then you should be required by law to get therapy and some sort of meditative practice. Money can't buy happiness, but it does buy power. And with great power comes great responsibility! So stop fucking everything up!

Anyhoo, on the off chance that one of you reading this book becomes a millionaire, or plans on becoming a millionaire, I wanted to give you guys a couple bits and bobs of insight that might help.

People who have money save money. People who have money spend money. Both of these things are true. One is a necessity, and the other is a calculated risk. If you know me in my waking life, you know that I spend very little money on material things. In fact, my greatest expense is . . . well, food. It's an amazing feeling being able to walk through Whole

Foods and buy anything I want. It's amazing to be able to experiment with expensive cuts of beef or fresh fish. Walking through a grocery store without worrying about the expense is the greatest form of privilege I know. I love it. I love it so goddamn much.

So! What are some ways to set yourself up on a money-saving path that could eventually lead you to a money-spending life? I'll tell ya a couple tricks of the trade.

If you're trying to work for yourself, or trying to start a creative venture, or trying to write a book that you're way behind on, make sure you charge all your devices the night before so that when you start your day nothing is standing in the way of you and your mojo.

Get a good night's sleep the night before.

Set up something in the evening that you look forward to that motivates your day.

And make yourself some overnight oats so you can be on your way with a body full of fuel and a vision for your future.

OVERNIGHT OATS

INGREDIENTS

Rolled oats

Milky milk (whatever strikes your fancy)

Yogurt

Honey

1. Confront your fear that this won't work or that it might turn out gross. Most of these ingredients come in bulk, so even if your first batch grosses you out or isn't what you expected, then just make another! Rolled oats aren't hard to come by, and you'll probably end up with way more than you need.

2. Get a jar that you can really seal. Like one of those fancy jars with the snappy metal clip and rubber around the lid.

3. Whisk together your ingredients in your preferred ratio into a bowl. There's not really a way to mess this up. You want your ratio to be like 3-2-1, milk-oats-yogurt/honey/etc.

4. Put it in the fridge and get your snooze on.

5. Wake up in a panic and rush out the door!!! Don't forget your oats!!

. . . And that's literally it. It's so simple, but it makes you really feel like you've done something for yourself. Plus, if you add a little flour, you could probably make a bad batch into cookies if you're not feeling like mush for breakfast the next day. Then it's cookies for breakfast! And that's amazing.

Long story short, save and spend wisely. Not just with your money, but also with your time.

JUNE

IN LOS ANGELES, THERE'S SOMETHING WE CALL "JUNE GLOOM."

It's a warm and cloudy time of year. The temperature is increasing, but the feeling of "summer" isn't quite there yet. It feels like one of those months that passes by too quickly, a month of transitions.

Around the world, June is widely recognized as "Pride Month"—the celebration of all things LGBTQIA+* and a time to recognize the sacrifices made by community leaders of the past. It's a celebration of queer culture and heritage. It's a time to rejoice for the rights that have been granted and to stand up for the rights that have been dismissed.

Pride has always been a complicated month for me. When you're raised with an attitude of homophobia, it's not something that's easy to shake. Even for someone like me, a queer leader in the public space.

This month of recipes will shed some light on the complicated matters of living "out loud and proud." I'll share my journey as a queer person and my observations on the journey our society is in the midst of . . .

And also we'll make a really complicated cake.

But first!

LET'S TALK ABOUT RAINBOWS.

* It's my personal preference to refer to my community as "queer" and to drop the acronym. So since this is my book . . . I'm going to say "queer" from this point forward. Doesn't mean you have to! Just letting you know that I am. :D

PRIDE: TASTE THE RAINBOW MONTH OF JUNE

PRIDE. Pride. Pride.

Sigh.

My relationship with Pride is complicated. I think it's complicated for two reasons.

The first being my relationship with the concept of "pride" itself. To feel proud. To feel proud of oneself, one's community, one's family, one's heritage, etc. I've always been stuck when it comes to the feeling of pride. Is it a feeling generated by a respect for one's history? For one's present? Why is it so easy for me to feel grateful but so hard for me to be proud?

I've done a lot of things that I should be proud of . . . and my feeling of self-worth is a work in progress. I've been trying to build it, to learn how to carry that inherent sense of worth with me throughout the day. To accept that by the simple act of living, I have worth. That worth isn't assigned by our actions, but instead assigned by the universal existence we call "life." Our lives have worth because we live them. This is the only chance we get. What more proof of worth could one need?

So in part, Pride for me means worth. Worth that I recognize. And, ideally, a worth that is recognized by others.

Which leads me to the second reason my relationship with Pride is complicated.

When you're part of a marginalized community, society tends to lump all of your needs into one. But that completely erases the experiences of the individuals in the group. And I'm not speaking to the experience of one person compared to another. I'm talking about the experiences of a trans person vs. a cisgender person. The experiences of a black person vs. a white person. A bisexual person vs. a gay person.

Obviously there are many similarities, and those similarities get recognized and receive attention. But what about the differences? Where is the room for our differences within our own community to be celebrated? Not just the differences our community has when placed in conjecture with heteronormative society?

When we fail to recognize and celebrate differences within the microcosm of the queer, we have failed to recognize each other's full humanity—and invite heterosexuals to do the same. We need to accept that the reality of someone else's existence doesn't disprove or discredit our own—even if the two are very different. I have hope, though. I figure if any community can get this right, it's ours.

So I guess the second thing Pride means to me is *hope*.

• • •

In many ways, the rainbow flag is the most fitting symbol for Pride because Pride itself means many things at once . . .

. . . So now that we've tasted the rainbow a bit, let's move forward into discussing the rainbow itself . . .

FLAG DAY: 6/14

THE RAINBOW WAS A SYMBOL THAT I LOVED AS A KID . . . UNTIL I FOUND OUT IT MEANT YOU WERE GAY.

I remember the moment it happened. I was in sixth grade. I found a rainbow pin at school and stuck it on my backpack. I've always loved solid colors. Never been a fan of patterns.

A friend of mine warned me that "rainbows mean you're gay," and being a homophobic lil' eleven-year-old, I immediately took the pin off and proclaimed how definitely not gay I was.

Methinks she doth protest too much.

• • •

In college, even after I came out, the rainbow was hard for me to like . . . I felt alienated by the queer community on campus because I wasn't as fully liberal and radical as they were. Not as angry. (Not in the same way, at least.)

The closer I stepped toward the community that was supposed to be mine, the further I felt from it. Being gay wasn't an

identity statement for me. It was just a part of who I am. Like the freckle on my nose. It's just my being; it's not my choice.

• • •

At thirty-two, I've found a way to love the rainbow again. I've found respect for the anger I once felt alienated by. I feel gratitude to those with the loudest voices and strongest identities because they made room for someone like me who was too meek to fight the fight on my own.

People call me brave, but I'm not the brave one. The brave ones are the people in the smallest towns or the broadest towns stretched over miles of freeway. The ones who live without access to diversity and culture and inclusion. The ones who are too young to live on their own and may choose to keep themselves safe in the closet, not out of shame but out of a conscious choice toward self-preservation.

I realize that the lack of comfort I initially felt from the queer community was because there was no comfort in myself. I was jealous of those who owned their identities. And for me, that jealousy manifested as a "pressure to be like them," which was all in my head.

I could be me if I let myself be. And the more you let yourself be you, the easier it is to allow others the same.

The Rainbow Cake pictured was a brain baby between myself and the amazing food stylist who worked with me on this book. A fellow homo, even! She made my dreams come true by making this beautiful muted cake. Out of ice cream! Wow!

So out of pure appreciation, I'd like to share my platform with Nora and give you guys the real recipe of how she made this cake come to be:

RAINBOW CAKE

INGREDIENTS

2 pints each of the six colors of the rainbow (or whatever colored pattern you want to create)

1. Spray two 9-inch springform pans with nonstick cooking spray. Line the bottoms and sides with parchment paper, leaving a 2-inch collar extending over the tops. Transfer pans to freezer.

2. Scoop the purple ice cream/sorbet into the bowl of a stand mixer fitted with the paddle attachment. Beat on medium speed until softened and spreadable but not melted, about 2 minutes. Transfer to one prepared pan and smooth top. Return to freezer and freeze until firm, about 2 hours. Repeat with yellow ice cream/sorbet in the second pan.

3. Continue process of softening, layering, and freezing with remaining colors, layering blue on top of purple and green on top of blue in the first pan, and layering orange on top of yellow and red on top of orange in the second pan.

4. To assemble, carefully release ice cream cakes from springform pans. Remove parchment collars. Using a large spatula, carefully transfer red-orange-yellow layer onto green-blue-purple layer. Return to freezer until ready to serve. Leaving the assembled cake on top of the springform pan's metal round will be easiest! Top with meringues or other desired garnish, slice into wedges, and serve.

{ NOTE THAT FREEZING TIMES MAY VARY GREATLY DEPENDING ON YOUR FREEZER. }

FATHER'S DAY:
THIRD SUNDAY OF THE MONTH

I SAT DOWN VERY PREPARED AND EXCITED TO WRITE THIS ESSAY. But then, when I went to title it, I was reminded that it was for the holiday Father's Day.

We have so many ideas of what the role of a father means when really we just need ideas of what the role of a parent means. Once I had a friend tell me that her father—who sadly passed away when she was young—would always remind her mother that "our children are not our property" and that they weren't obligated to return any of the "favors" of parenting through their actions.

I find this thought very comforting. That instead of our children growing inside rigid identities that we control, they create their own identities as a reflection of their makeup and our mentorship. It's a combination of factors, including culture, community, and commitment. Parents can put so much energy into their children (positive, negative, etc.), but what is energy without balance?

• • •

When I first learned there were "four elements" in life, I spent hours trying to come up with more. Earth, wind, water, fire . . . ? . . . That can't be all, right? What about metal? What's metal?

COLD
HOT

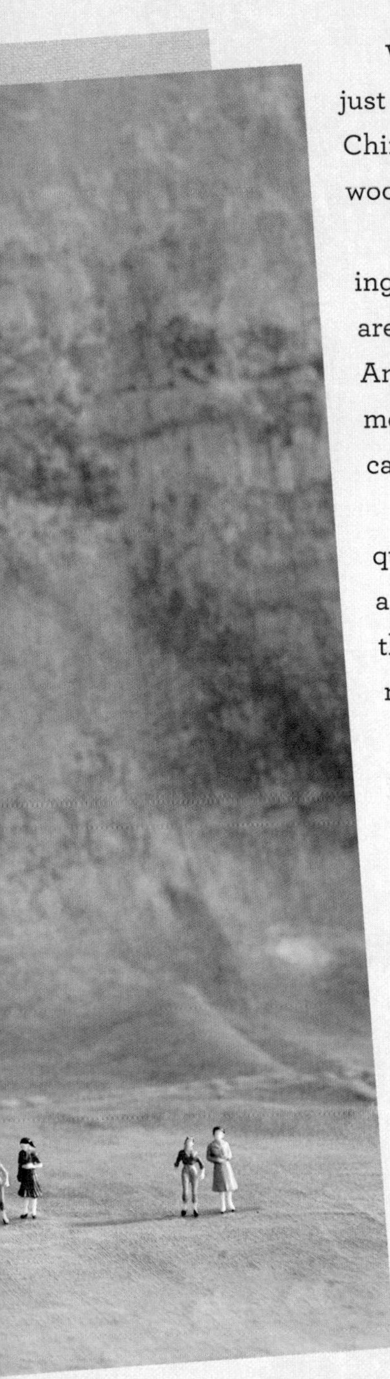

Well, it turns out that metal is an element, just not one that's a part of Western practice. In Chinese medicine there are five elements: earth, wood, water, fire, and metal.

Now if you're like me you might be wondering . . . Hey, wait, where is the air element? And aren't "earth" and "wood" basically the same? And what is a metal . . . like gold? What's a diamond in this equation . . . earth? Because it's carbon?

And if you're still like me, after all these questions your next thought will be . . . Listen, after five thousand years of existence, I'm sure these ancient practices probably know a little more than I do.

And now is the part where I transition to how this is related to food and Father's Day and get back to the point of this being a "cookbook" at all.

The five elements of Chinese medicine seek to find a balance, taking into consideration everyone's natural predispositions to have more of one than another. For instance, I'm a person with "excess fire," which probably means I shouldn't drink, but ya know what, I'm having a glass of wine right now and that's suiting me just fine.

What was I saying? Ah yes, balance.

So much of cooking involves balance. A balance of flavors on the palate. A balance of portions on the plate. A balance of the budget as you try and treat yourself to a fancy meal or two. A well-trained chef has learned enough of their own balancing act to be able to taste a soup and note that, ah, it needs more citrus, not more salt.

To gain this sense and skill, one has to spend years experimenting with finding that balance. And balance doesn't have to be equal. It just means (or rather *I* just mean) achieving synergy in alignment with your goals.

Which leads me back to Father's Day. And the household itself.

The idea of parenting roles being designated by gender is outdated not only because it isolates women from more "masculine" roles but also because it isolates men from more "feminine" roles.

Each person has their own set of strengths and weaknesses. Their own set of reliefs and stressors. To form a happy household, partners must trust each other to see who they are and what they need. To know when their partner needs a little more citrus and a little less salt.

TL;DR—EACH PERSON HAS THEIR OWN MAKEUP. KNOW YOURS TO KNOW WHAT KIND OF FOODS YOU SHOULD BE EATING FOR GREATER BALANCE AND LONGEVITY! OR NOT!

THE FIVE ELEMENTS

(OR WHO THEY WOULD BE AT A HOUSE PARTY)

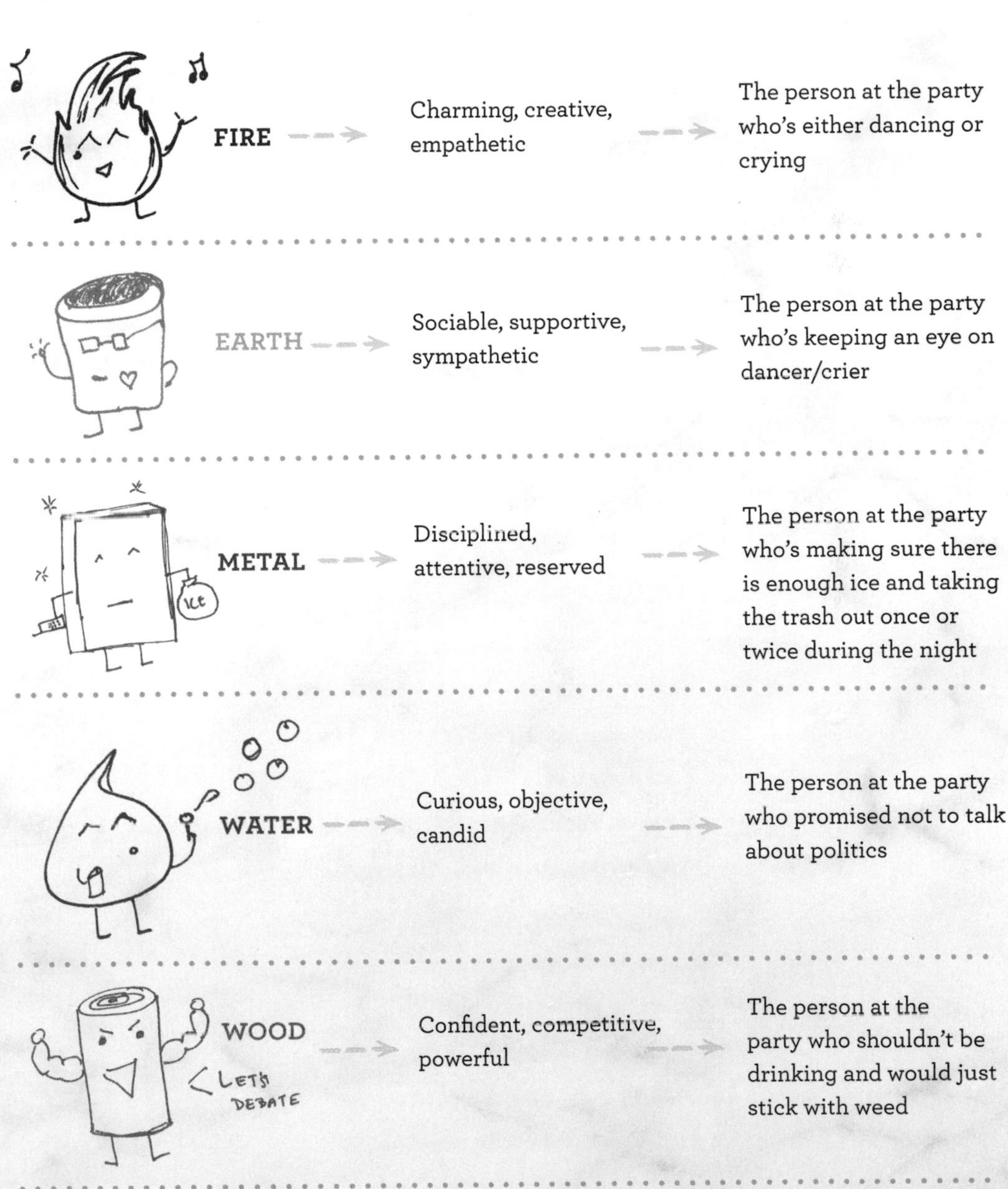

FIRE	Charming, creative, empathetic	The person at the party who's either dancing or crying
EARTH	Sociable, supportive, sympathetic	The person at the party who's keeping an eye on dancer/crier
METAL	Disciplined, attentive, reserved	The person at the party who's making sure there is enough ice and taking the trash out once or twice during the night
WATER	Curious, objective, candid	The person at the party who promised not to talk about politics
WOOD	Confident, competitive, powerful	The person at the party who shouldn't be drinking and would just stick with weed

SUMMER SOLSTICE: 6/21

THE SUMMER SOLSTICE IS THE LONGEST DAY OF THE YEAR AND THE SHORTEST NIGHT. And if you're looking for a reason to celebrate something, then you're in good company! Cultures across the globe have been celebrating the summer solstice for years: In ancient China, the summer solstice was observed to celebrate earth and other "yin" forces. In ancient Rome, it was to celebrate Vesta, goddess of the hearth. (Interesting because we Western cultures think of "the hearth" as being a very winterly thing.)

For our summer solstice celebration, we are going to be making something ancient and spiritual . . . mead! Here are the puns I thought of for this:

- **More than Meads the Eye**
- **Get Ready to Mead Your Maker**
- **The Meading of Life**
- **Mead and Greet**
- **What Does the Summer Solstice Mead to You?**
- **Don't Live Beyond Your Meads**
- **By All Meads Fair**
- **By Any Meads Necessary**
- **He's Got a Mead Streak**
- **What's That Supposed to Mead?**
- **Yes Meads Yes and No Meads No**
- **The End Justifies the Meads**

DO NOT
DISTURB

So engage in a pagan ritual of your choosing and let's get down to business by making some mead!

MEAD YOUR MAKER

INGREDIENTS

Honey

Water

Yeast (NOT baking yeast!—must be a brewing yeast)

. . . And that's it!

Optional: add some flavor friends (cinnamon, nutmeg, ginger, etc.)

NOTE: INGREDIENTS ARE THE EASY PART. IN THIS SEEMINGLY SIMPLE RECIPE, YOU'RE GOING TO NEED A BUNCH OF SPECIFIC TOOLS FOR THE JOB, MOST IMPORTANTLY A THERMOMETER TO WATCH YOUR TEMPS AND SOMETHING TO SIPHON YOUR MEAD WITH. THINK OF IT LIKE A SCIENCE EXPERIMENT. SCIENCE AND MAGIC ARE INTERCHANGEABLE DURING THE SUMMER SOLSTICE—WHEN SCIENCE IS MAGIC!

1. Figure out what style of mead you wanna make—that directly influences your water-to-honey ratio. For instance, if you want a softer mead, for 1 gallon of water, you want about 1 pound of honey. And if you want a really sweet (barely drinkable) mead, then you can do 5 pounds of honey per gallon of water. But yuck.

2. STERILIZE EVERYTHING. When experimenting with home brewing, you want to avoid anything that could turn your batch to vinegar. Usually it's bacteria. So clean everything with boiling water and then get started.

3. Boil water again! (This boil is when you add your flavor friends, if you're doing the master class of mead making. For me, I'm just happy enough to boil water.)

4. Remove water from heat and stir in your honey. You're almost there!

5. Cover mead mix and let cool to the temperature of a human body. The recipe I was using for reference says "Blood Temperature," which I think sounds so witchy and cool.

6. Boil a cup of water and mix in a tablespoon of honey. Let it cool to BLOOD TEMPERATURE again and then add your yeast.

7. Let that sit overnight.

8. Go out and dance naked in the moonlight while your yeast does its dirty magic.

9. The next day combine your yeast mix and your mead mix. Now you're making mead! Which involves a lot of patience.

10. Cover for a few days, come back, say "EW!" and then siphon it into a new clean container to leave any bits you don't want behind. Fermentation isn't pretty. But sure is tasty! This is the step that involves you using whatever your stylish sealable container will be.

11. SEAL YOUR MEAD and let it ferment for about a month in a warm, dry place.

12. AGE YOUR MEAD and store it in a cool place.

13. GIVE YOUR MEAD TO A FRIEND because you're too scared to try it yourself. But make them open it in front of you. Be ready to drive them to the hospital if something has gone terribly wrong.

14. Sage the room to get rid of the spirit of your dead friend.

15. Say, "My bad!" if the spirit manifests before you at night when you sleep.

16. Repeat yearly until you get the hang of it.

JULY

I USED TO REALLY DISLIKE THE SUMMER MONTHS.

But now I like them! The end! Yay!

Oh, wait. I need to say more than that? Books have words, you say? More than just pictures? Sheesh, if you say so. We are halfway through the year—cut me some slack.

Speaking of cutting slack—let's talk about politicians. They don't deserve any slack cut. It's crazy to think that by the time this book comes out, we will have presidential nominees. Are you registered to vote? You should check on that. Even if you're sure you are. My voter-registration status changed last year. I was very disturbed by it. That's why I always like to mail my ballot in.

Voting is a right. And a privilege. It's both. It's something you've gotta do. No matter how busy or tired you are. We must vote and participate in politics. Otherwise we end up with . . .

WELL, YOU KNOW WHO.

INDEPENDENCE DAY: 7/4

AMERICA! What a confusing and wonderful place!

My relationship with my home country is a fickle one. On one hand, I'm proud to be an American, born in the USA. But on the other hand, I'm horrified by how divided we are as a nation. I can't help but think that the solution lies somewhere in conversation. Coming together in a productive dialogue seems to be something we as a people struggle with—and when it comes to our leaders, the struggle seems even harder.

Think of the schoolyard bully. They come off brash, garish, full of confidence and fury. Children experience this as if the bully was born that way and it's simply their nature. Wiser parents know that many bullies at home are just repeating what they've seen at home. So if our political atmosphere is one of bullying, then what example does that set for the children of the nation?

Conflict can be cured through conversation. Conversation and communication are harder than ever during this time when temperatures have risen such. People are so willing to come to violence as a form of solution and a perceived act of strength—but I can think of nothing that takes more strength than having constructive, compassionate discourse with someone who doesn't share your beliefs.

Which begs the question . . . is there a way for something so separate to come together and be whole again?

Yes. As an example of constructive discourse and dividing and reuniting, I'll describe making some deviled eggs.

DEVILED EGGS

INGREDIENTS

Eggs

Dijon mustard

Apple cider vinegar

1. Take your eggs and bring them to a boil for about 12–14 minutes. Depends on your eggs, your stove, your pot, etc. Always consider the factors that are particular to you.

2. Put your eggs in time-out by gently placing each one into an ice bath. Ask them to listen to each other and think about what it is they hope to say, and what they fear the other thinks of them.

3. Carefully peel off the shells of each one, listening to all their fears and complaints.

4. Now that all the eggs are laid bare, slice them and remove the cooked yolks. Consider how similar we all look on the inside.

5. Take the yolks of their ideas and combine to taste using a smattering of your favorite seasonings or condiments. For me it's Dijon and a little bit of apple cider vinegar to give it some sweetness.

6. Scoop the yolk of your combined understanding out of the bowl and place back into the whites of the eggs.

7. Hope that through some calm, vulnerable time spent together, these eggs will walk away with their own individuality but paired with a sense of unity.

8. . . . And now eat them.

ICE CREAM DAY:

THIRD SUNDAY OF THE MONTH

YOU CAN DO IT, HANNAH! You are perfectly capable of typing things. Even second drafts of things. Which might even be your third time thinking about these things. You are perfectly capable of writing this book.

The above paragraph I usually delete after I've finished writing a recipe, but for this particular recipe, I've decided to leave it in, because for me Ice Cream Day is all about giving ice cream a second chance. You see, many moons ago I tried to make ice cream from scratch. A very foolish endeavor, but I was a child of twenty-four and ready to take the world by storm.

Back then, I had only seven "internet cooking videos" under my belt. I was far from being a chef, or comedian, or, well, anything, really. Back in 2011, being a "YouTuber" wasn't a thing, so I was mostly a young adult posting videos of herself drinking and cooking on the internet and hoping this wouldn't later destroy her future employability. I wavered a lot about whether it was something that was really worth doing at all.

One person in particular was a huge champion of my con-

Stir in Some Love
Always Handled with Care
From Our Family to Yours
Power of We

tinued video-making—my older sister, Naomi. She watched every video I made and gave me notes to incorporate before uploading. Her main note often being "not funny," or, even worse to me, "not you." She instilled in me the importance of authenticity. She liked "Hannah" being "Hannah," not "Hannah" trying to be a comedian or trying to be . . . well, frankly, anything. She wanted a Hannah just trying to be herself. Online. While drinking and cooking. A tall order, to be honest.

I was living in New York then and taking the train to DC to spend time with Naomi and her husband on the weekends. We were rascals in our twenties with just enough of an age gap for me to feel completely at ease. I was with my big sister, so no matter what, I was going to be taken care of.

To this day that episode of *My Drunk Kitchen* (the eighth episode of the whole series) remains my all-time favorite and also the drunkest I have ever been in a kitchen. I think waking up with chicken nuggets on your chest, lying in a puddle of melty goo really sticks with a person.

Now if you're thinking, "But, Hannah, how does this relate to *me*? What am I supposed to be getting out of this story? Where's my lesson?" Well, I encourage you to follow the recipe—the same recipe that I tried to make—and see where your lesson lies. Full disclosure: The ingredients are simple. The instructions even more so. So take a gamble and celebrate Ice Cream Day by facing simplicity head on. What does it bring out in you?

ICE CREAM

INGREDIENTS

Milk

Sugar

Vanilla

Ice

Rock salt

1. Take your milk, sugar, and vanilla and put them into a quart-size zippered plastic bag. SEAL IT LIKE YOU'VE NEVER SEALED A BAG BEFORE. (This will be very important later.) Hell, maybe even double bag it for now.

2. Take a gallon-size plastic zippered bag thing* and fill it with ice. Then pour in your rock salt. A lot of rock salt, as much as you think you need to keep the ice from melting. (Some recipes say 8 tablespoons will suffice.)

3. Put the small bag in the big bag.

4. Shake your groove thang.

5. Shake shake shake.

6. Twist and shout!

7. Do the hokey-pokey!

8. Work out for the first time in months . . . with the bag!

9. Pray that the second, smaller bag hasn't broken open . . .

10. . . . Ah, crap.

11. Just go out for ice cream. You've earned it.

* Can you tell how hard I'm trying to avoid saying "Ziploc"?

HOT DOG DAY: 7/17

HOT DIGGITY DOG! Look at all these beautiful wieners!

. . . Wait, that didn't sound right at all.

Today is Hot Dog Day, so it's time to throw a sausage party!

. . . Wait, that doesn't sound right either.

Celebrate by sliding these thick, slick meat tubes between your buns!

. . . It's only getting worse. I give up.

HOT DOGS

INGREDIENTS

You don't really wanna know what's in a hot dog. Just buy some and leave it at that.

1. I mean, there are so many ways to make a great hot dog. Here are some variations you might enjoy:

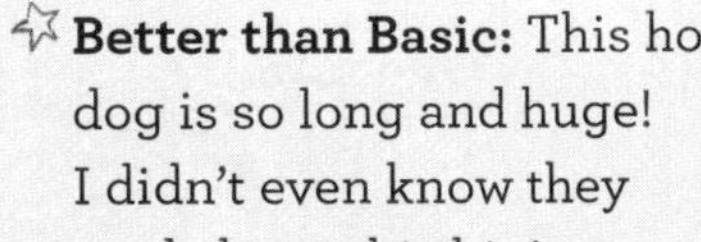

- **Better than Basic:** This hot dog is so long and huge! I didn't even know they made buns this big!
- **Corn Dog:** Put your doggie on a stick, make a corn batter, dip, fry, rejoice.
- **Kielbasa (my fave):** Have a pool party with some friends. Mysteriously disappear for a moment, only to reappear with a freshly grilled kielbasa and some toothpicks. You'll be a hero.
- **Overachiever:** If you look closely, you can see that the bun is also grilled. Hot damn.
- **Wrapped in a Blanket:** You're on a roll! (A crescent roll, that is.)
- **In a Potato with Sauerkraut and Pickled Onions:** Because . . . why not?

HERRADURA

LIPSTICK DAY: 7/29

OH MY GOD, YOU'RE GORGEOUS.

Sorry, got distracted.

Ahem.

Let's talk about beauty. No, not the "unrelenting standards" or "Photoshop ideals" of beauty that plague society today. Let's not talk about the wealth factor of those who get to remain "young" and "healthy" and "beautiful" because they have the money and the time to devote to the pursuits of these things.

I'm serious. Let's not talk about it. (Right now.)

Because there is a lot I've learned from Beauty.* There's a lot I've gained by having pride in my physical appearance. There are so many people who've shown me Beauty through their unrelenting confidence and self-acceptance. It's not about shapes, sizes, or colors. It's about feeling safe, confident, and comfortable. These attitudes in combination are beautiful to me.

* Capital *B* meaning the Beauty Industry.

So in honor of Lipstick Day, let's put our social concerns on hold and celebrate beauty a bit.

Here is a fun drink to drink while playing with makeup on Lipstick Day. Ooh, maybe even throw a party! All genders are invited to celebrate Lipstick Day and play with makeup! Oh my goodness, wouldn't it be amazing if this holiday was recognized by all and this is how it was celebrated? I would really get on board with that. The change starts with us. Here and now. This is not a moment; it's a movement.

Actually . . . it's a margarita.

WATERMELON MARG

INGREDIENTS

Tequila (mezcal if ya like it smoky)

Limes

Watermelon

Basil

Sugar

Ice

1. Make a basil simple syrup. Melt sugar in water and infuse with basil. That's all!

2. Make a lime-heavy watermelon margarita.

3. Oh, you want more details than that? Okayyyyy . . .

4. Call your friend and ask them if they want margaritas. When they say yes, say, "Me too! Where should we go?"

5. Just kidding againnnnn . . .

6. Here is how you make a margarita: combine tequila, salt, lime juice, and watermelon in a blender. Blend with ice. Sip as you go. Add more mezcal to yours. Drink up and get back to the gossip you were so thoroughly enjoying!

AU-
GUST

AH, AUGUST.

August is a funny sort of month, isn't it? I remember growing up with the sense of August having a twinge of finality. Summer was ending. School would return soon enough. But just because summer is almost over doesn't mean we can't give it the grand send-off that it deserves! Why should we just let August pass us by when this forgotten month of summer includes many holidays deserving of our attention and celebration.

The next month includes recipes for the overlooked and somewhat neglected. Holidays that celebrate the underdog or, in one case, specifically the dog!

(This is where I would try and make a pun about the dog days of summer . . . but the joke seems too obvious to be in this book full of wit, wisdom, and now . . . woof.)

So sit back, relax, and contemplate the woes of the forgotten as we leave the traces of summer behind: Middle Child's Day, Left-Hander's Day, Just Because Day, and . . .

DOG DAY.

MIDDLE CHILD'S DAY: 8/12

EVERY TIME SOMEONE WITH SIBLINGS TELLS ME THEIR BIRTH ORDER (OLDEST, MIDDLE, YOUNGEST), I LIKE TO GO, "OHHH . . . THAT MAKES A LOT OF SENSE." To which they usually reply, "REALLY???" And I usually say, "Oh, definitely." Because everyone likes to have a sense of place, and I'm sure to some extent it's true that they are a product of their placement in their order of siblings whether or not it applies on a larger scale to all siblings in similar roles.

Or maybe I say it because I'm too accommodating.

And maybe I'm accommodating because I'm the middle child.

But I wasn't always the middle child. I spent over a decade being the youngest before our youngest sister was born. Which eventually led to her adoption into another family, which gained me two more siblings, this time brothers, one older and one younger. In this new grouping of five . . . I was still exactly in the middle.

Frankly, I love being the middle child. It's kind of like the best of both worlds! You get to learn responsibility while not being solely responsible. You get to be whiny and needy while not being the whiniest or neediest. It's a fun little role being in the middle. You can duck under everyone's gaze . . . or be roped into being the most helpful.

When I've done reading about "middle children," I haven't really found anything that's struck a chord. They often talk about them being "pessimistic" or "resentful" and "acting out," as if middle children have an internalized lack of attention. That's nuts! I don't constantly crave attention!*

I think if there's any defining statement I would make about being a middle child based off my personal experiences, it would be about the "preciousness of objects." I always wrote my name on things or named them after myself. My teddy bear was "Hannah Bear"; my plastic doll would be "Hannah Doll."

I think it was this sense of possessiveness (or, in a positive light, "ownership") that might be my most defining middle-child characteristic. Not that I don't love to share. I very happily share most things. Ella often complains that when people come over to our apartment they leave with stuff they probably didn't even want. To which I scoff and say, "If they didn't want it, they should have said no—not yes!" To which she tries to explain to me "subtle social cues."

Pfft.

Anyhoo, the point of this is to say that not enough credit goes to middle children for being the most middle. Being a middle child means absorbing and defining roles within preexisting dynamics (older) and the novelty of the new (younger).

Which is why Middle Child's Day should have its own designated celebratory snack! For this snack I've chosen the blintz.

Why the blintz? Here's why.

A blintz is basically a crepe that's rolled, filled, and drizzled with something new. A crepe is like the older sibling. All knowing and haughty. The filling is what makes the middle sibling themselves. The drizzle is the younger sibling stealing the show.

* Said the entertainer.

BLINTZ, BABY

INGREDIENTS

Eggs

Flour

Water

Milk

Vegetable oil

Sugar

Salt

Vanilla

Ricotta

Lemon zest

Berries to make a berry-based sauce

1. Make some blintz puns to get yourself in the mood. "Don't be such a basic blintz."* "Let's get blintz'd." "That's blintz, baby!" "Don't blintz twice!" "Talk about a BLINTZ-krieg . . . Oh, wait, that's a luft-WAFFLE."

2. Make a crepe. Which you already know how to make because you've done it once before (older child), so maybe you don't need to pay as much attention the second time.

3. Decide on a filling. Are you feeling a ricotta moment? Wanna blend it with a little cream cheese for an extra bit of tang? Go for it! This blintz is here to be your sloppy seconds anyway. You never even knew if you wanted children!

4. . . . You love children, actually. And you love this blintz. Which is why you're going to go above and beyond on your berry sauce and make it from scratch. You're an ambitious parent with a renewed zeal for parenting. Now it's time to go above and beyond and give this topping everything it deserves!

* What's wrong with being basic, anyway?

At the end of the day when you look back at your blintz baby, you'll see that every part relied on the others. The crepe-like pancake provided the initial structure, the filling provided the substance, and that sweet berry sauce brought it all together and made every bite feel new again.

A middle child—much like the filling in the blintz—is usually your favorite part. But you just can't tell from looking at it.

LEFT
meatless
Just

» LEFT-HANDER'S DAY: «

8/13

"STUDIES" SHOW THAT 10 PERCENT OF THE WORLD IS LEFT-HANDED. I want you to think of ten people you know. Are any of them left-handed? If not, then you might want to think about whether you have any hidden biases you might want to address.

Another study (conducted by me on my Twitter) shows that 20 percent of the people who follow me on Twitter are left-handed! I like to think this is because they know they are welcomed and accepted.

Imagine living in a world where everything was slightly (and then sometimes not so slightly) more difficult. And then if you brought it up to people, they were like "Prove it!" or "That's not my experience of X."

So if society can make room enough to acknowledge that some people need left-handed scissors, then I personally think there's a lot of hope and progress ahead for becoming more racially aware.

DOG DAY: 8/26

FULL DISCLOSURE: I DON'T OWN A DOG.

However, I do love dogs. In the same way that I love all God's creatures: objectively and from afar.

Look, I get the bond between a dog and its owner. I really do. They are like little furry children. They are blunt and loving and needy and take big poops. Just like a baby does. But at the end of the day . . . a dog isn't a baby . . . but it *is* something that you need to keep alive. Just like a baby! Wow. The parallels are endless.

As your friend, I want you to keep your dog alive. Thus, in honor of Dog Day, I think you should make a meal that you and your dog can share. To help get that started, I've compiled a list of all the things you eat that are safe for dogs and another list of foods that could potentially kill your dog (one time I saw someone feed a dog a potato chip, so honestly, I just don't really know—if you're in doubt, you should look it up), which is the opposite of what you want. Even as a cat-lover, I can understand that.

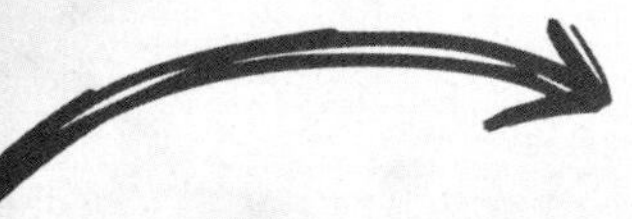

FOODS THAT ARE SAFE FOR DOGS:

- APPLES (NO SEEDS)
- BANANAS
- BEEF
- BLUEBERRIES
- BREAD
- CARROTS
- CELERY
- CHICKEN (COOKED, NO BONES)
- CORN
- EGGS (COOKED)
- FISH (COOKED, NO BONES)
- MUSHROOMS
- OATMEAL

- PEANUT BUTTER
- PLAIN YOGURT (NO SUGAR, NO SWEETENER)
- PORK (COOKED, NO BONES)
- QUINOA
- RICE
- SALMON (COOKED)
- SHRIMP (COOKED)
- STRAWBERRIES
- SWEET POTATOES
- TUNA
- TURKEY (COOKED, NO BONES)

And that's it! . . . According to this one website I found.

HERE IS A MUCH SCARIER LIST OF THINGS YOU DEFINITELY SHOULD NOT BE FEEDING YOUR PUP:

- ALCOHOL
- CAFFEINE
- CHOCOLATE
- GARLIC
- GRAPES/RAISINS
- MACADAMIA NUTS
- ONIONS

That first one sure is a bummer, right? Wouldn't it be great if you could share a Pimm's with your pooch?

JUST BECAUSE DAY: 8/27

WE'VE SPENT A LOT OF TIME TALKING ABOUT BEGINNINGS. How to motivate ourselves. How to be proud of ourselves. How to take on new perspectives. How to start your at-home doomsday-bunker kit.

For a moment, though, I'd like to talk about endings.

Just because.

Because everything starts and stops, because a pendulum swings both ways, because knowing yourself isn't based off theory; it's based off fact.

And the fact of the matter is that I'm in my thirties now and I just can't drink like I used to. And that's okay. I think. I hope?

Addiction runs in my family, so I've always watched myself closely. And I've scared myself from time to time as well. It's hard when something that is so toxic for the body and the brain is also so socially acceptable. Alcohol should be treated as an indulgence. And when you think about it, it's mind-blowing that it isn't. What if after work everyone always went out for ice cream instead of happy hour? That would be . . . too much ice cream. So what are our options? Does this mean we all have to just sit around drinking tea and meditating? That seems boring! (But also sounds lovely if it was something that was easy to do.)

Lemme reset.

One of the hardest parts of transitioning out of your twenties and into your thirties . . . it's kind of like letting go of your adolescence. Except now we're letting go of adultolescence instead. And even writing that breaks my heart because I miss my twenties self. I miss the energy, the enthusiasm, the possibility, the hope. The newness of a life that was lived as my own. Now, even with the incredibly fabulous life I have today, the fatigue of adulthood is something I can't escape. And those who continue to chase life with the same youthful abandon end up seeming stunted and, at their worst, stunting others.

So here are some facts you're going to have to accept about drinking in your twenties versus your thirties:

- You can't drink like you're in your twenties.
- It will be harder to lose weight.
- It will be harder to get excited.
- It will be harder to have hobbies.
- You will feel more self-conscious.
- Time will pass quickly and casually, like a pickpocket taking all your best intentions.
- Some of your friends won't be friends anymore.
- Some of your friends won't be here anymore.

All these factors come together to make one thing abundantly clear: You need to take care of yourself. And I'm sorry because it's so exhausting. And I'm sorry that you don't want to do it anymore. And I'm sorry that you're hoping that someone, someday, will just step in and do it for you.

There will be people who surround you to share your load. Or to bear witness to your burdens even if they are yours alone. There is company. You create company.

There is a point to this.

And that point is:

It's okay to take yourself more seriously. It's hard. Oftentimes embarrassing. But it will become bearable. It is bearable. And it beats the alternative.

Don't ignore your changing needs. Don't ignore your changing self. Don't ignore the fact that you might not be able to be the person you are used to being. That you may need to lean on them more than you'd like to. That's understandable! You have back problems!

Anyway, this is just to say that I'm rooting for you. I really am. Because you've been there to root for me. The best thing I can do is be honest.

You must grow. So grow slowly. No one is angry at a flower creeping up a vine. It's not the path it takes or the shape of its roots. It's what blossoms.

Just make sure what blossoms is you.

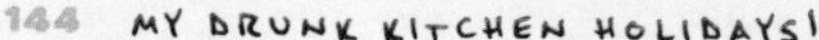

SEPTEMBER

SEPTEMBER! THE TUESDAY OF MONTHS!

September is the first month where the Holidays (with a capital *H*) are in sight. September is a month of beginnings and endings, as the new school year looms ahead and summer draws to a close. The holidays in September reflect this feeling of in-between-ness. I say September is like a Tuesday because Tuesday is the day of the week that feels long, but also daunting because there is so much week left ahead.

September is an oddball month whose holidays reflect its scattered nature. We have Labor Day, which grants us some time off from work or school that has just now started again. We have Cheese Pizza Day, which is a blessing since "bikini season" is now officially over (not that it really ever started anyway).

And then we have some outliers like Video Game Day and Love People Day, which feel like they don't require much education or celebration.

But ignore all that because this book is about finding smart and sustainable ways to celebrate all year long! And buckle up with these friendly reminders of self-care and appreciation because the *real* Holidays are comin' at ya FAST.

ENJOY!

LABOR DAY:
FIRST MONDAY OF THE MONTH

"STOP GOING TO THE DOG PARK AND HAVE A BABY ALREADY!" This is a text message I just received from my mother, who has been asking me to get pregnant and have a baby since my early twenties. Her intention is good. Protective, actually. In her mind, having a baby is a form of life insurance. A form of social security. Having a child means that you'll be loved unconditionally. That you'll be taken care of and looked after.

Unfortunately, that's the role of the *parent*. Not the child. But a fair amount of people seem to have this dynamic backward in their heads.

In my family, most of the children grew up "parentalized," meaning that they are the primary caretakers of the household. My goal in this life is to get all my "child-ing" out of my system *before* I become a parent. I want to be the giver of unconditional love to my child. And if they grow up to hate me for some reason, well, that's their right. From my perspective, the obligation is one-way. My job is to love them forever, no matter what. To be a grounded and constant force in their lives. Children are not given to you to make up for the sins of your parents, so don't relive *your* childhood during *theirs*.

Having a baby is about being prepared to be the second most important thing in your life. For the rest of your life. So better give it some practice first.

Experience can be the greatest teacher. So for those of us who won't ever be pregnant, how can we truly understand and share in the experience? Well, by strapping a watermelon to our bodies, of course!

HOW TO STRAP A WATERMELON TO YOUR BODY USING DUCT TAPE

INGREDIENTS

Watermelon

Duct tape

1. Ask for help. No man is an island. Takes a village. Et cetera.

2. While holding the watermelon against your body, support the weight with your own two hands. These are the fundamental resources you'll need to maintain to start your life as a parent. This is the lowest the bar can go.

3. With the support of your community (meaning the one friend you convinced to come over here and help do this ridiculous thing), begin attaching the duct tape on the bottom third of the watermelon, wrapping back around your waist. You want the low-hanging support first.

4. Next it's time to do the top third. Hopefully you're wearing a tank top of some kind, because pulling this much duct tape off your skin is going to hurt. That's like labor itself. Predictably (extremely) painful.

5. Proceed with your day as planned. Try to live the life you've known but now with this extra weight you will have to carry. After the baby is

NOTE: OBVIOUSLY THIS IS NOTHING LIKE BEING PREGNANT, BUT WHO WOULDN'T WANNA SEE THEIR SIGNIFICANT OTHER TRY TO CLEAN THE HOUSE WITH A GIANT WATERMELON BABY? FUN FOR THE WHOLE FAMILY!

born, this weight becomes emotional. Make sure that you've been taking care of your mental health and building up the personal strength to support this weight. You'll be doing it for the rest of your life.

When it comes to having children, or when to have children, my stance is one of patience. I am excited to be a mother one day, but I want to do it when we have the emotional excess to support another member of the family. It's a big deal. It's not an obligatory life stage. Humanity is overpopulated. Having a child is an honor, a privilege, and a choice. Make sure to treat it as such.

CHEESE PIZZA DAY: 9/5

COLLEGE IS FOR FUN. Your twenties aren't.

(And if you're currently in your twenties and thinking that college isn't fun—well, you are in for a RUDE awakening.)

Your twenties risk becoming the decade of putting things off because you think you'll have time in your thirties to figure it all out. Well, here is a heads-up: If you picture yourself owning a house in your thirties, it's because you bought it in your twenties or early thirties.

If you picture yourself married in your thirties, it's because you spent your twenties exploring your wants, wishes, and worries about partnership.

If you picture yourself as an executive or working your dream job in your thirties, it's because you spent your twenties sacrificing in that direction.

• • •

So in honor of Cheese Pizza Day, and realizing that your defining decade is here, let's make ourselves a slice of all the things we shouldn't have anymore!

(LACK OF) INGREDIENTS

Everything you love

JK

But for real

Top Ramen

Beer

Pizza

Mac and cheese

All chips

Energy drinks

Okay, but for real . . .

POSTCOLLEGE COOKING ADVICE

INGREDIENTS (AKA STAPLES TO HAVE SO YOU DON'T STARVE)

Eggs

Cheese

Tortillas

BEANS

Powdered soups!

(*continued on next page*)

1. Realize that when you go to your parents' home and say there is "nothing to eat," you actually mean "Oh my God, Mom, there is so much to eat, what a completely full fridge, I am going to eat so much while I'm here."

2. Eggs are your best friend. They are little pockets of protein that come in so many forms. (See March, Egg Blessings.)

3. Melt cheese on something. It will taste good. Do this enough times and people will start calling you a chef.

Slightly fancier Top Ramen

Eggs

Mainly, eggs

4. Remember that your baby brain is still growing, so try and find a way to get some omegas in there. Your brain will be fully baked once you're twenty-five. (Or if you live in any state with legalized marijuana, your mind can be fully baked by eighteen. Eyyyyyy.)

5. Consider buying fruits and/or vegetables. Decide against it and buy Bagel Bites instead.

6. Consider buying *frozen* fruit and/or vegetables. Realize this is a good investment because it can double as an ice pack. Credit yourself for being the genius you are.

7. Get some green tea and drink one cup a day. Couldn't hurt.

NOTE: THERE IS NO CHEESE PIZZA RECIPE HERE BECAUSE . . . WELL, BECAUSE I DIDN'T WRITE ONE. IT'S A PIZZA, PLUS TOMATO SAUCE, PLUS CHEESE. YOU'RE WELCOME!

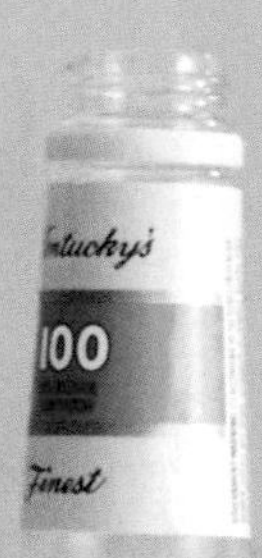
100
Finest

Simpler Times
PILSNER
50% ALC/VOL
(100 PROOF)
Top Ramen
Anatomy and Physiology

VIDEO GAMES DAY: 9/12

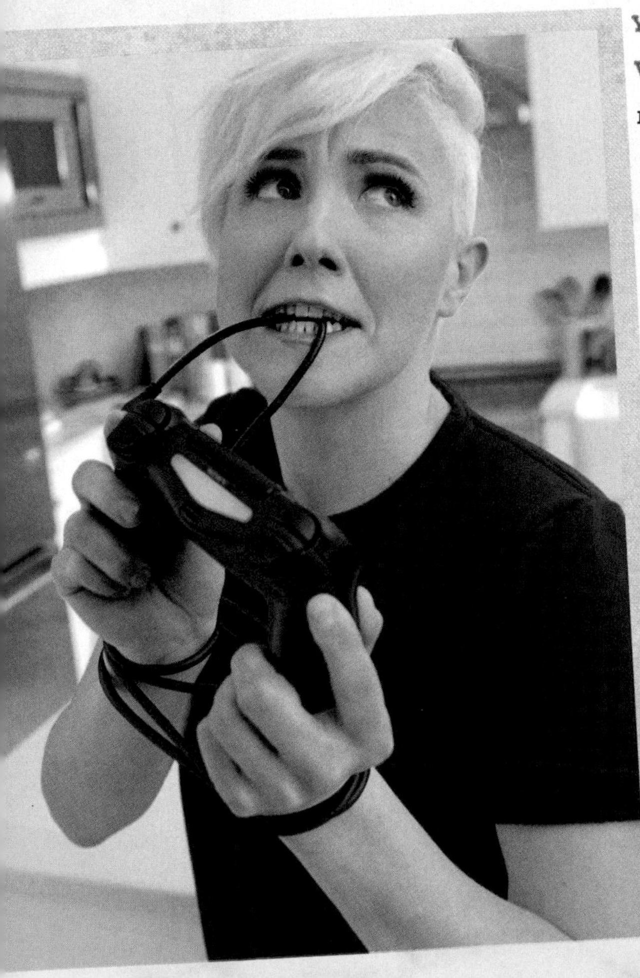

YOU MIGHT THINK MY GREATEST VICE IS ALCOHOL.* Or maybe even my love for the NFL.** But really it's my gluttonous relationship with video games.

I would not describe myself as someone with any self-control or discipline. This isn't something to brag about. It's also the source of my broken self-esteem. Because in my mind, if someone has self-discipline, then they are unstoppable. And I am very stoppable. Incredibly stoppable.

Except when it comes to video games.

I feel like video games are . . . pretty dangerous for someone with addictive tendencies. One time I played *Best Fiends* for eight hours. Think about that. It's an app. I just

* So I still cannot spell "alcohol" correctly on the first try. I've concluded that I'm just from a parallel universe where "alcohol" is spelled "alchohol."

** You might be right.

couldn't stop. When I play a video game, it's like starting a book that you just have to finish. Except at the end of a good book, you feel a sense of completion. At the end of a video game (if that game does in fact have an ending), I just blink and think:

"Wait . . . what was I doing?"

It comes down to the difference between entertainment and escape. Unfortunately, I feel like all forms of entertainment are an escape for me. What truly relaxes me is making things. But it's hard to make things. So I don't relax. Boo-hoo, woe is me.

• • •

So, let's be honest here. I'm going to keep playing video games. But I might as well eat healthy snacks and feel marginally better about the whole thing.

LIST O' SNACKS THAT WON'T DESTROY YOUR BODY (IMMEDIATELY)

- **Carrots**
- **Roasted Unsalted Almonds**
- **Cherries (with pits! It's a great way to occupy your mouth while staying focused!)**
- **Jicama with chili and lime**
- **Cold cucumber with chili and lime**
- **A frickin' apple**
- **Pistachios**

NOTE: ALL SNACKS GOTTA BE CRUNCHY BECAUSE YOU'RE BUSY BEING A GAMER AND NEED TO STAY ON IT.

We all have our vices. It's important to accept yours for what they are and to accommodate accordingly. Love to snack while gaming? That's okay. Just put healthy options in front of you. Also, get up and stretch. And make sure you're getting some sun. Also . . . please shower.

LOVE PEOPLE DAY: 9/30

MAN. People. Am I right?

I love people, though. I really do. Right now, as I write this, the waitress at the café where I'm writing is comparing her forearm to a customer's. I have no idea what they are talking about. Maybe sleeves. Maybe arm length. Maybe skin color. Maybe hair. Who knows? But they are both smiling and laughing and sharing a moment that neither will likely remember. They are both smiling as the customer departs, smiling for different reasons or for the same, but it's the kind of smile that's so soft it can't be anything other than sincere.

Anyway, there is a lot to love about people. There's a lot to fear. There's a lot to protect. There's a lot. People are a lot.

And I'm one of those people! And I can be a lot. For instance, I don't eat pork. And people always reply with the exact same question: "Not even BACON?"

And I say no, not even bacon.

So here is something that fulfills the crispy, greasy umami of bacon. You can still eat bacon. I just don't. And that's the biggest part of loving people. It's letting them be. As long as it doesn't hurt you, then just let them be.

You be you. And I'll be me.

So here is my recipe for kale chips!

KALE CHIPS

INGREDIENTS

Kale

Lemon

Salt

Pepper

Olive oil

1. Come to terms with the fact that you're about to make kale chips. Something that prior to 2010 I'm pretty sure didn't exist. The future is weird.

2. Pull out a flat baking sheet. Wonder why it's still dirty. Ignore the corners and just put wax paper over it. Those things never get clean. Everybody knows that.

3. Oh, damn, do you even have kale?

4. Wait a week until the next farmers' market, because if you're gonna make kale chips, you might as well commit and go all the way.

5. Rinse your kale and break it off into bite-size pieces.

6. Pour olive oil and lemon and salt and pepper over the kale. Stick your hands into it. Doesn't that feel amazing? The kale is so thick and coarse, and yet it's also so supple. My God. Is this what religion feels like? Because this is worship to me.

7. Bake at 350 degrees for 10–15 minutes, shaking halfway through. Turn up the heat for

a sec if you want it crispy. Or raise it up a rack. Oven make hot. You decide the rest.

8. Take your "chips" out and squeeze a bunch of lemon on top.

9. Put them back in.

10. JK, TAKE THEM OUT AGAIN, I was just seeing if you were paying attention.

11. Eat and enjoy! You're getting your daily dose of fiber right here and now, so don't be alarmed at the newfound regularity of your bowels.

People are also frustrating.

I would like to encourage you to make room for people and their differences. Some of us don't eat pork and yes, that means even bacon.

P.S. THE WAITRESS I MENTIONED BEFORE CAME BY AND GAVE ME A WHOLE CARAFE OF GREEN TEA. WITHOUT ME ASKING. WOW. PEOPLE, MAN.

OC-
TO-
BER

Here we are on month ten of the year!

We've been building up confidence, working through our doubts, but now maybe it's time to address some fears. After all, another year is approaching its end, and there are still two months left ahead. So maybe now it's time to admit what we are afraid of to make room for all the gratitude and gift giving to come.

Halloween was one of my favorite holidays as a kid. Not because of the candy, or the costumes, or any of the spooky stuff. Frankly, I was (and am) a scaredy-cat. I don't enjoy horror movies. I don't like to plummet down on a roller coaster. I'm not a thrill seeker by any stretch of the imagination. I feel like my resting state has plenty of adrenaline in it and have no desire to increase this amount.

But despite all this, I loved Halloween as a kid. I loved the faint chill in the air. The sight of summer's final sunsets. The cozy, crisp sound of leaves crunching under my feet. During Halloween I got to enjoy all these things and do something that's rare for any kid raised by a single parent: We all got to do it together. It's a shared activity that turns the neighborhood into a household. Everyone is oohing and aahing over each other in shared celebration. For families that aren't going to have a bountiful Thanksgiving or a lavish Christmas, Halloween takes its place as the anticipated centerpiece of the fall. Children and adults become equal. And I suppose, as a child who felt very much like an adult . . . I thought Halloween made a lot of sense. It was fun.

So! The following recipes are my attempt to share a little bit of that fun with you. Even if you (like me) don't love to spook or be spooked, there's something sentimental and sweet in the month ahead that's just for you. Starting with some of my favorite nocturnal companions . . .

MENTAL HEALTH DAY: 10/10

SO.

There are many, many things I can say about cats. Cats can be just as playful as dogs. Cats can be just as social as dogs. Cats love you. Cats love you so damn much!

Ultimately, I feel like cats are deeply misunderstood.

For instance, black cats representing bad fortune? That's bonkers! Did you know that people with cats were less likely to get rodent-driven diseases like the plague?!*

There is one cat in particular that I love a whole helluva lot. His name is Charles and he is my baby boy.

And one time he almost died.

• • •

Having pets as an adult is scary. Having pets in general is scary. However, when you're in early adulthood, you're finally ready (somewhat) to begin taking care of yourself, and may even take on another living creature! But do it carefully. A pet is like a practice baby and should be treated as such.

Ella and I only decided to get a pet together after a great deal of debate. She and I both switched sides about it in equal turn. Weighing the pros and cons, considering my travel schedule, considering her work, considering the amount of

* Look, do I have a source for that? No. But does it make total sense? Yes. More cats = less rats. I'm an epidemiologist now.

physical space we had, considering considerations. A lot of talk. A lot of thought. But ultimately, a lot of want. And I really, *really* wanted a cat.

So we decided to get a cat for my thirtieth birthday, in November. We saw Charles, and there was no room for debate. We ended up getting a cat in May.

Charles was fifteen weeks old and came to us via airplane. He was a slightly hairy "hairless" cat, so the people who had original signed up to buy him backed out. Ella and I jumped in and boom. We became parents.

I was away when Charles arrived. But we became inseparable the moment Ella picked me up from the airport with him in the car.

When you work from home, it's easy to get to know your cat. And to get to know your cat fast. Charles is my only coworker. And he's a damn distracting one.

During the first week, Charles played and pranced and destroyed every beloved paper product we had.

Ten days into having Charles, I noticed that he seemed . . . uncomfortable? He wouldn't play, he wouldn't prance, he would just shake his head like a twitch and then bury his face into me. Then—to my horror—one of his eyes would dilate while the other would remain still. It was honestly . . . pretty creepy.

Anyway, I took him to the vet and they said he had an eye problem and gave me the card of an ophthalmologist. I said, "Are you sure? Because it doesn't seem like an eye problem, it seems like an eye symptom." They politely listened and then told me to try and get in touch with the ophthalmologist in the next couple weeks.

The next morning, Charles woke up with blood coming out of his ear.

I went to the ER and made a big scene, Charles almost

died, his brain was under pressure due to swelling from a dual ear infection, we got him antibiotics and drained his head. He may or may not have brain damage, but we'll never be able to truly know. He seems fine to me!

Long story short, he's allergic to chicken.

RAW BEEF AND SALMON FOR CATS

1. Get raw beef
2. Get raw salmon
3. . . . Blend?
4. Nevermind.

We feed our kitty babies raw beef and salmon, but I would never dare to make it myself. There are plenty of companies that make small-batch food for pets if you can spare the buck.

FUTURE BRIDE, ELLA!

FREETHOUGHT DAY: 10/12

IN THE FIRST FOUR MONTHS OF MY RELATIONSHIP WITH FUTURE BRIDE ELLA, WE SHARED OUR CONCERNS ABOUT FAMILY, INTIMACY, HOME, AND EVENTUALLY SHE REVEALED HER GROWING CONCERN THAT I WAS ACTUALLY A VAMPIRE. So to celebrate Freethought Day, I wanted to tell you guys the story and also treat you to a tasty pasta dish.

Now, it wasn't the sort of thing that came up in a teasing, joking way. It was a legitimate fear that she had finally confessed when we were walking back to the car one night from dinner . . .

"Look at that moon. It's huge! A gentle reminder of our place in space. More gentle than the sun, ya know? The moon welcomes us. It feels warm to me. When I look at it, ya know? It's warm."

"Mm-hmm." Ella's response was quiet as we walked back to the car. Our conversations swing between quiet and constant. When Ella talks, it's often without ceasing, almost as if she is composing and conveying the thought all at once. Getting it all out before she loses it. Other times, she's quiet and contemplative. She doesn't reveal a lot, she doesn't share information unprompted, she's a bit of a mystery, but in a way that's welcoming, not intimidating. She keeps to herself much like the

moon, present but distant. Who knows what mysteries lie beyond the depths of those dark brown eyes . . .

"Are you a vampire?"

. . . And then sometimes I realize I have no idea what she's thinking about.

"Ha! I wish! Ya know, when I was a kid, I actually spent the majority of sixth grade thinking I was a vampire. I even went through a very brief 'goth' phase where I wore sunglasses at night and dressed in all black. It ended when my mother and sister couldn't contain their laughter once when I got into the car. Embarrassment is middle school's greatest teacher . . . Is it this one? I think we have one more block."

Ella was listening intently. I could feel her eyes on me as we walked looking for the car. Being the center of attention is a marvelous thing. She must have picked up on my subtle cues when talking about my childhood. So empathetic! So wise.

"So are you?"

"Am I?"

"Are you a vampire?"

"Ha! Who knows . . . I guess time will tell, right? What do you think you are? Maybe you're a fairy."

It was easy for me to picture Ella as a woodland fairy. She's got long, wavy brown hair. And an intimidating resting face punctuated by an open laugh and joyous smile. Seems like she's a fairy to me.

I turned to look toward her and noticed she was looking a bit panicked.

"Are you a vampire? How do you know you're not? Oh my God."

I was laughing now. "Ella! Are you seriously asking me this? Where is this coming from?"

"Well, the morning after our first date, you left in the

middle of the night!" Jesus. That was months ago. She's been thinking of this since then?

"Technically, it wasn't the middle of the night, but yes, it was very early in the predawn morning."

Our date had gone on longer than expected, and it had been so wonderful that it startled me a bit. I was working on boundaries, so waking up with Ella at my apartment felt like a step backward into old, destructive patterns. I panicked, and it was too early to take a walk, so I took a drive instead. I came back around 7:30 to find Ella awake, and we went out to breakfast. Simple enough.

". . . And there were NO mirrors in your house . . ."

Fair. But is that so weird? I had just moved and didn't really use mirrors. Usually if I had an event, someone was coming to do my hair and makeup, so why would I need a bunch of mirrors. And there *was* one mirror; it was just not very large and it was in the bathroom and it wasn't hung up . . . but I guess waking up in a stranger's house alone would be enough to make someone's mind look for any indication of danger.

". . . You're super strong . . . which is weird because you're small . . ."

What can I say?

". . . And you're always pointing out weird things like bats . . . and you're always awake at night . . . and you're so pale and you listen to classical music! Who listens to classical music?!"

She's not wrong about those things. But does that a vampire make? At this point we had found the car and were standing outside it finishing our conversation before we got in. She reminded me of Hermione Granger (my secret closeted crush while reading *Harry Potter* as a kid). Here she was talking about the supernatural, but really she was the one casting her spell on me.

"Well?"

I was the one who had been quiet this time.

"Well . . . I mean, who knows! How do people really know things?"

"Oh my God, Hannah! Jesus. Just say it! Oh my God, what if you really are a vampire . . . oh my God." Ella was clearly genuinely concerned.

"I can't be a vampire. Remember when I made you dinner last week? We talked about how much we both loved garlic. I kept adding cloves and we bonded over . . . Wait a minute . . . Is that why you were being so weird about the garlic? Were you thinking about this?!"

Ella nodded emphatically, and I laughed and kissed her. I have always been told that I was a weirdo, but now I had a weirdo of my very own. Vampire or not, I was ready for the eternity that would be this life we shared together.

We got in the car and the classical music came on. Ella pointed at the radio, and I switched it to jazz, which she declared was not much better. We shared our supernatural thoughts and all the beliefs in magic that we held as children, and even the ones we secretly carried as adults. We fell into a comfortable silence, driving back to my apartment, guided by the light of the waxing moon. In the moment, I was falling in love with her.

Ella broke the silence with a declaration of her own.

"It's okay if you're a vampire. Just promise that you'll tell me."

"I promise."

It's my belief that the idea of garlic warding off the feared and the foul stems more from its medicinal properties. Garlic helps with digestion, it purifies the blood, and it fights infection; it's really a wonderful little member of the onion family.

PASTA FROM THE HEART (OF A NON-VAMPIRE)

INGREDIENTS

Spaghetti for two

Your best olive oil to impress a lady

Fresh garlic, as many cloves as you'd like

Cracked red pepper

A little bit of Parmesan

Lemon (for zesting or squeezing)

Salt

Pepper

1. Boil your water and add your pasta for the allotted time it takes to cook. Most spaghettis are 8–12 minutes, but honestly, if you're boiling it for 12 minutes, that's just too long. So do it for a healthy 9 minutes.

2. During those 9 minutes, sauté some garlic with olive oil in a pan. If you slice it, it will burn and become crispy. So chop it up real fine and add it as close as you can get to the end of that 9-minute mark. (Optional: You can add your cracked red pepper here too if you're feeling like a crispy time!)

3. Take your pot off the heat. Scoop some spaghetti out and start adding it to your sauté pan. Add a little of the starchy water from the pot if the pan looks like it's burning. Add a little more olive oil if you're really panicking.

4. Salt, pep, you know the drill.

5. Take it off the heat and put it directly into a bowl to serve. Add your pepper and your cheese, squeeze a little lemon, and serve. It's okay to feel proud. You cooked a meal, dammit! I'm proud of you too! You've got the energy because night is falling soon. Uh . . . not that you're a vampire.

FOR AESTHETIC PURPOSES, IT NEVER HURTS TO ADD A LITTLE GREEN. PARSLEY OR BASIL ARE GOOD OPTIONS DEPENDING ON WHAT YOU'RE FEELIN'.

COLOR DAY: 10/22

HAPPY COLOR DAY! Let's talk about synesthesia! JK.

But it IS Color Day! So let's celebrate with an ode to colors during this color-changing time of year by making as beautiful and rich a color as we can.

Isn't it amazing that red is a primary color? Really think about that. What are primary colors? They are the ONLY colors that can't be made by combining other colors together. Which is wild to me. I mean, how do we really know that they can't be made and that they just exist? Isn't all of existence something being made out of other somethings? Which came first, the chicken or the egg? Why are we here?!?

These are some scary thoughts. Good thing it's October. Time to get spooky-ooky.

CANDIED APPLES

INGREDIENTS

Apples

A leeeeeetle bit of corn syrup (sorry)

Hella sugar

Red food coloring

Vanilla (for flavor, but who are we kidding, no one is gonna eat this)

Branches from neighbors who are cool with you grabbing some branches (or your own tree if you have a house and/or yard)

1. Go to the grocery store and get super red apples. Don't worry about freshness since they are a year old anyway. (All grocery store apples usually are. Isn't that wild?!)

2. Pull branch off a tree. Insert branch into apple. Contemplate the irony of it being plucked from a tree, only to be speared by another branch. *Très* Frankenstein. Very fitting for the holiday.

3. Start making your coating. Sugar, corn syrup, water. Heat slowly. Stir mucho.

4. Once that starts to boil, grab a candy thermometer . . . from the store . . . ahead of time. Oops, should have mentioned earlier that you're going to need one.

5. Remove from heat. Add food coloring. Add vanilla. (Or skip. I truly doubt that anyone is going to eat this.)

6. Put your hand upon your hip. When I dip, you dip, we dip. (The apples, that is.)

7. Place on plate and feel accomplished!

NOTE: IF YOU WANT TO DO THE COOL DRIZZLE EFFECT, THEN JUST DIP INTO YOUR LEFTOVER CANDY MIX WITH A SPOON, AND TRACE IT OVER THE TOP. IF THAT MAKES SENSE. MAYBE GOOGLE "CANDY ANGEL TEARS" AND WATCH A VIDEO THAT EXPLAINS BETTER. THANKS FOR BUYING THIS BOOK, THOUGH!

HALLOWEEN: 10/31

AS I MENTIONED BEFORE, MY FAVORITE PART OF HALLOWEEN IS THE CONCEPT OF "THE NEIGHBORHOOD."

I don't know my neighbors. Maybe this is because I'm not a homeowner. And I don't have kids yet. So what is Halloween? Well, it's a costume party with a slightly spooky theme.

The idea of having a neighborhood—the idea that the people against the wall opposite of yours have any care about what they hear through it—really appeals to me. We live in an apartment building. Our neighbors hear us fight, we hear them fight, and then every time we see each other everyone just looks at their phones. Or if by accident we make eye contact, then we smile.

But the idea of having a *neighborhood* is so appealing to me. Everyone has different careers, different lives, different causes and effects that led them to this home by chance. Somehow, we've ended up next door to each other. Living entirely separate lives within intimate proximity.

So I guess what I'm trying to say is that Halloween is a time to take a chance. A chance on a costume, a chance on hosting, a chance on somebody.

(I guess, now that I think about it, the risk factor is pretty high . . . because what if your neighbors are creepy? And then you open your door and your hospitality and they end up

being . . . not great. Neighbors aren't friends. They are people who happen to live next door. Hmm. I've come full circle on this whole thing. Don't invite your neighbors over. Instead just give them a Starbucks card with a note apologizing because you're going to have some people over and it might be a late night.)

Anyway, here's a recipe for some spicy smoky margz:

SMOKING SPICY POTION

INGREDIENTS

Something dark, tart, and mysterious—just like you

Tequila (mezcal is the hip new thing, babyyyy)

Citrus (probz a lime, let's be real)

Ice

Some sort of herby simple syrup ("herb" is the word)

Dry ice (most "magic" is just dry ice anyway)

1. Make a margarita! This means taking ice, tequila, citrus, and sweet and mixing them all together. Don't blend this kind, though, because . . .

2. . . . You'll need to add something dark and tart, like a tart cherry or a hibiscus. That gives it that rich purple color that just screams "I put effort into this!" If you blend it you're going to diffuse your colors, so just serve it over rocks.

3. Then make a "smoky" margarita bar so people can add their own smoky elements. Maybe smoky means like chili, maybe it means something more cinnamony, maybe it means a smoked-salt rim. Any of the above! Think of a Bloody Mary bar, but make it spookier and more margarita compatible.

4. Bask in the compliments of your friends and family! Stay classy, though. Don't gloat. (In front of them.)

A GRATITUDE ATTITUDE

DESPITE ITS OBJECTIONABLE ORIGINS, THANKSGIVING IS MY FAVORITE HOLIDAY.

Or rather, the spirit of Thanksgiving is my favorite holiday spirit. Thanksgiving is about gratitude. Now, a message of gratitude can sometimes be overdelivered. Especially if you frequent the self-help spaces as often as I do.

I don't take issue with the message of gratitude or the importance of gratitude. But I do take issue with the lack of instruction on how to bring more gratitude into yourself and your life. Without the tools to do so, how are you supposed to truly be grateful? It's more complicated than just "making sure you say you're thankful"—gratitude is a reflective action. And in our forward-forward-forward world, reflecting backward is not an instinct we learn.

Gratitude is also a connective action. To be grateful, you need to be able to see the connections, the cause and the effect. For example, the other day I was standing in line at a café I'd never been to before. I was in a hurry to write, and so

I planned on just getting my standard order and not spending time browsing the menu—the menu, by the way, looked amazing, and I can't wait to get back there and take my time next time.

As I approached the front of the line, the lady in front of me stepped to the side and said, "Go ahead, I'm going to take forever to order."

Given that I was in a hurry, given that I was eager to get seated and get to writing, I was deeply grateful in the moment. She would never know the extent of it—I told her "Thank you!" and "That's nice" and that was all. In that moment I think I figured out that gratitude is an entirely internal experience. *Appreciation* is the action. *Appreciation* is the gesture made for the sake of conveying something to another. I always conflated the two, but I see now how different they are.

Gratitude is a private experience. It's feeling that you're not alone. That someone has your back. That someone—for no reason at all—decided to make things a little easier for you. That somebody sees you.

So, I'd like to take this moment to say that I am *grateful* for the opportunity to share these thoughts with you all. And I *appreciate* your giving this book a chance. I hope it's been as tasty a trip for you as it's been for me.

Now! Let's get to the good stuff. Over the next couple pages, you'll find some frankly straightforward recipes. I want to share with you guys my four essential Thanksgiving dishes. Sure, there's a lot more that goes into the meal, but for me and my family, these four dishes are a must. Since it's my favorite holiday and this is my book, I'm going to give it all the attention it deserves!

Without further ado! Let's celebrate the things we are grateful for.

PRO TIP: BUY EXTRA THYME, ROSEMARY, DILL, LEMONS, GARLIC, AND ANY OTHER FLAVOR FRIEND THAT YOU REALLY ENJOY. EVERY RECIPE THAT INCLUDES THEM COULD PROBABLY BENEFIT FROM INCLUDING SLIGHTLY MORE.

WARNING: THIS IS
AN UNGODLY
AMOUNT OF
GARLIC.
ONLY ATTEMPT
IT IF YOU'RE NOT
A VAMPIRE . . .
OR IF YOU'RE A
VAMPIRE WHO'S
IMMUNE TO
GARLIC.

GARLIC-ASS MASHED POTATOES

MASHED POTATOES ARE THE BEST WAY TO SERVE POTATOES. There. I said it. Yeah, come at me, bro! Are you going to argue that french fries are better? Well, yes, they are! However, it's not a dish that proudly declares itself as a "potato," is it? French fries and tater tots may pass as more masterful tasty bites, but I am proud to support a potato that does not turn away from its roots!*

* Did you know that a potato is NOT a root vegetable despite the fact that it grows underground? It's actually a *stem* vegetable. Because it has buds and sprouts and leaves. So it's not the root . . . it's the stem. A potato is more closely related to rhubarb than a radish, more celery than carrot. Fascinating, right?

INGREDIENTS

Cream or milk (depending on how brave you're feeling)

Hella garlic

Potatoez

Salt

Butter (probably)

Olive oil

Look, I'm not out here trying to tell you how to make mashed potatoes. It's not an exact science and it mostly derives from personal preference and texture. The basics are to peel (or not), to cut (or not), and to boil. While boiling . . .

1. Take some bulbs (yes, that's right, BULBS, not cloves) and slice off the tops. Then drizzle with olive oil and bake at 400 degrees. It doesn't matter how many bulbs you do because this is Thanksgiving and as far as I'm concerned every dish can be improved with the addition of more garlic.

2. Drain your mashed potatoes and start mashing!

3. Add some butter.

4. Mash, mash, mash.

5. Add some salt.

6. Mash, mash, mash.

7. Add your cream (or milk).

8. Mash, mash, mash!!

9. Take your garlic out of the oven, squeezing each full bulb into your mashed potato masterpiece.

10. If you don't think your mashed potatoes are thick enough, then simply turn the heat up and keep mashing and stirring. This will evaporate moisture and thicken your goods. But STAY FOCUSED. Because burned bottoms are a quick way to ruin a great potato dish. (Or improve it. I'm not here to judge.)

11. Keep going, and add salt and pepper to taste. Add more garlic, even. Once you get to the point where you can't stop "tasting" it to make sure it's good . . . that's when you know you're ready to serve.

A GREAT GRAVY

GRAVY, GRAVY, GRAVY. I love gravy. In my opinion, it's not Thanksgiving without gravy. Also, it's the only time of year I ever have it! Probably because cooking an entire turkey is the essential part of the recipe. And it's not like I find myself baking big birds all year round.

Gravy is the grandparent of the Thanksgiving meal. Gravy is the inheritance. A good gravy, or gravy just the way you like it, feels like tradition in a tablespoon. Every family has their own take on a gravy—store-bought or otherwise. Here's ours:

INGREDIENTS

Turkey bird for baking, buddy!

Rosemary

Thyme

Sage

Onion

Celery tops

Flour

Salt

Pepper

Cold water

1. Bake a bird, baby! It's important that you're baking a turkey on a pan that you can also make your gravy in—this is where you'll be placing your base broth after your bird is done.

2. While turkey is baking, place neck and giblets in water with a bundle of rosemary, thyme, and sage with a chopped onion and top ends of celery. Simmer within reason. If you're baking a massive bird for eight hours, then no, don't simmer the whole time. You get it.

3. Remove turkey from the pan. Add broth from above and bring to a slow, wide boil. A large rectangular pan works for this—it can occupy the space over two burners.

4. In a jar, place a couple of tablespoons of flour with salt and pepper.

5. Add 1/2 cup of cold water and shake well! This is a great job for any sort of family

member who seems eager for a task but can be given no real responsibility, because come on.

6. Add mixture to boiling drippings and broth. Stir until it thickens. Strain if you want to.

7. Place into familial gravy boat—if you don't have one, then just anything will do.

A NOTE ABOUT THE BOAT: HOW COOL WOULD IT BE TO HAVE THINGS YOU CAN PASS DOWN TO YOUR KIDS? WE NEVER HAD THINGS LIKE GRAVY BOATS GROWING UP. SENTIMENTAL OBJECTS ARE RARELY USEFUL. BUT A GRAVY BOAT CAN BE BOTH USEFUL AND SENTIMENTAL! I THINK I'VE JUST REALIZED HOW MUCH I WANT ONE. MAYBE I SHOULD TAKE A POTTERY CLASS AND TRY TO MAKE ONE. WOW. THANK YOU, THANKSGIVING. YOU'RE THE GIFT THAT JUST KEEPS GIVING.

GREEN BEAN CASSEROLE

GREEN BEAN CASSEROLE IS A DISH THAT GRANDPARENTS LOVE AND PARENTS HATE. At least for my generation. And the reason behind this has to do with the dawn of canned goods. Green bean casserole started out in 1950 as a can-on-can dish. Canned green beans + canned cream of mushroom soup + French onions and ya done. It's a simple, kinda nasty dish.

From the canned era, green bean casserole moved on to the frozen + semi-canned era. It became *frozen* green beans + canned cream of mushroom soup + French onions and ya done.

As for me and my budding family, we like to make green bean casserole in the most time-consuming way possible: from scratch. Wait! Don't go anywhere! It'll be worth it, I promise. And once you've done it once, it will start to get done faster and faster. Or at least it will seem that way. Because of how the brain processes memory.*

Enjoy!

* Time and memory are formed together. New experiences feel longer. Then shorter. And then longer again. I'm a neuroscientist now, FYI.

INGREDIENTS

Fresh green beans

Kosher salt

Olive oil

Cremini mushrooms, sliced

Unsalted butter

Hella thyme

Flour

Milk

Heavy cream

Hella garlic

Fried onions

Grated Parmesan

Salt

Pepper

1. Get your oven ready by setting it to 375 degrees. You're going to have to be careful with your timing! Most of Thanksgiving is about timing. Think about it like an intricate dance. The kind of dancing that makes you sweaty and stressed out . . .

2. Boil green beans in salt water until cooked but still crunchy. Like an *al dente* pasta.

3. Drain and set to the side so they have some time to chill out and reflect.

4. Next sauté your cremini mushrooms in olive oil. If you're feeling ambitious and want to play with texture, you can cook the mushrooms on one side and then the other. This is a marvelously ambitious task and no one will notice, but I noticed, and now I am praising you for it—WELL DONE!

5. Add butter. Add thyme.

6. Cook them all together until the mushrooms are a texture you enjoy, then put them to the side to cool.

7. Make a roux! What's a roux? It's flour and butter. And milk. And cream. Look, it's hard to do. The internet can tell you! Probably far better than I can . . . but basically I would say that it should end up looking like the base of a creamy sauce.

8. OMG, you've made your roux into a béchamel.* Holy hell, you're a cooking god!

*** Béchamel is like a roux that goes super saijin.**

9. Now that your sauce is thick and bubbling, slice up your garlic and add it in with salt and pepper.

10. OH GOD, IT'S BURNING, this is why you should slice your garlic beforehand!

11. Put your green beans in a casserole dish.

12. Pour your sauce over it.

13. Cover with foil and bake for 25-ish minutes. Better under than over!

IMPORTANT NOTE: THE FINAL STEP IS TO UNCOVER AND BAKE FOR AN ADDITIONAL 15 MINUTES OR SO. IF YOU'RE ATTEMPTING TO COOK A THANKSGIVING FEAST, THEN DO THIS CLOSER TO THE ACTUAL DINNERTIME. YOU CAN PREP YOUR CASSEROLE LONG BEFORE YOU GIVE IT ITS FINAL BAKE. ONCE YOU DO, THEN TOP IT WITH CRISPY CRISPIES (THAT'S THE FRIED ONION) AND PARMESAN AND CALL IT A DAY!

The best part of making this dish is that it's a conversation starter. I promise. If you bring up "green bean casserole" to any older generation, you are guaranteed to hear a great story.

Optional: if you have gizzards from turkey, boil these until they are cooked and take out of water and chop up into small pieces and add to the veggies mixture before you add the bread cubes.

Or you can add chopped apples, walnuts, hazelnuts, and/or other dried fruit if you want.

BLACK OLIVE STUFFING

ELLA MAKES THE STUFFING IN OUR FAMILY. Technically it's a dressing. When I asked her for the recipe, she sent me this. I don't know why it's in ALL CAPS, but it came from her mom, so that makes some sense to me.

INGREDIENTS

BOX OF MRS. CUBBISON BREAD CUBES (ANY ONE IS FINE)

3 OR 4 RIBS OF CELERY

2 OR 3 GREEN BELL PEPPERS

2 YELLOW ONIONS

1 LARGE CAN OF SLICED BLACK OLIVES

1 LARGE BOX OF CHICKEN BROTH (LOW SODIUM AND ORGANIC IS BEST)

SEASONING: SALT, BLACK PEPPER, GARLIC POWDER OR GARLIC SALT, ONION SALT, THYME

CANOLA OIL AND 1 STICK OF UNSALTED BUTTER TO SAUTE THE VEGGIES

1. WASH CELERY, TAKE OFF THE BOTTOM PART (WHITE-ISH) AND THE TOPS. CUT RIBS IN HALF, THEN LENGTHWISE INTO STRIPS. CUT STRIPS INTO SMALL CUBES. CHOP ONIONS AND BELL PEPPERS INTO SMALL CUBES ALSO. PUT ALL INTO A BOWL AND SET ASIDE.

2. HEAT A (PREFERABLY) NONSTICK PAN AND ADD ABOUT A TABLESPOON OF OIL AND ABOUT HALF OF THE BUTTER (YOU CAN ALSO JUST SAUTE WITH THE BUTTER AND SKIP THE OIL). ADD VEGGIES AND SAUTE UNTIL ONIONS ARE TRANSLUCENT. (DO NOT BROWN THE ONIONS OR VEGGIES!) SEASON TO TASTE AND ADD OLIVES. STIR-FRY FOR JUST A FEW MINUTES.

3. PUT SAUTED VEGGIES BACK INTO A LARGE BOWL FOR MIXING. ADD 1 BAG OF THE BREAD CUBES AND SLOWLY ADD BROTH; YOU MAY WANT TO ADD THE SECOND BAG DEPENDING ON HOW MANY VEGGIES YOU HAVE—THERE SHOULD BE AN EVEN RATIO OF VEGGIES TO BREAD. YOU JUST WANT TO MOISTEN THE MIXTURE WITH THE BROTH, NOT SOAK IT. SHOULD HAVE THE CONSISTENCY OF A WET SPONGE AND NO LIQUID VISIBLE, JUST WET MIXTURE. REMEMBER TO KEEP TASTING FOR SEASONING BEFORE YOU BAKE IT . . . !

4. PUT THE MIXTURE IN A BUTTERED BAKING DISH, ADD A FEW PIECES OF BUTTER ON TOP, AND BAKE FOR ABOUT 30–45 MINUTES TILL GOLDEN BROWN.

DE-
CEM-
BER

CONGRATULATIONS!

You've made it to December. The most mournful/joyful time of year. December is a month packed with presents and presence. December is a time of great nostalgia. And honestly, it's a month that . . . makes me pretty sad. No matter what winter celebration you've inherited (Christmas, Hanukkah, Kwanzaa, Saturnalia, etc.), it comes with a boatload of memories: some good, some bad.

So what do you do with all those memories? Well, you examine them closely and bring with you the ones you wish to keep. Make your memories into new traditions. No matter the size or scale of your celebrations, they are your own. You can choose to do as you please. December is a time of family, even if it means that the only family you feel comfortable sharing it with is yourself.

Need to skip the holidays this year? Go for it! Take yourself on vacation.

Don't want to travel but do want to see everyone? Negotiate! Say you need everyone to come to you this year.

Can't wait to show up your hometown friends with your rabid success and fancy new Tesla? . . . Stay put. You're probably being an asshole.

No matter what your circumstance, use December as a month of reward and celebration. The following recipes are made to be shared. Gather yourself and your loved ones to your hearth. You've made it through another year!

AND YOU MADE IT THERE TOGETHER.

BEAR
ESSENTIALS

COOKIE DAY: 12/4

A COUPLE OF YEARS AGO, AT THE BEGINNING OF OUR RELATIONSHIP, ELLA AND I GOT INTO A TWO-HOUR DEBATE ABOUT THE AGE AT WHICH YOU TELL A CHILD THAT SANTA ISN'T REAL.* We were spending the weekend with my sister Maggie and were dropping her off at school at the time.

It was one of those conversations you might expect a couple who were preparing for children to have. But both Ella and I like to get ahead of things, so even though it was the first year of our relationship, we decided this was a debate that needed to happen that day. We were sitting at a pub in Boston, across the street from Maggie's campus, waiting as she finished a two-hour-long orientation. We both agreed that at some point we had to start calming down so that Maggie wouldn't be concerned when she came back. We're like parents already!

The most interesting part of the debate was the end. Basically, my argument was that we should tell the child as soon as they're old enough to ask. Ella's argument was to wait until later, although in the end, I think we realized we were talking about the same age—probably around second grade. But the

* OMG. I hope I didn't just reveal that to someone reading this book to their baby before bed at night. Seasonal spoilers! My bad!

most important part was remembering that we're both firm believers in magic, and we want to make sure our child knows that just because *Santa* isn't real doesn't mean *magic*'s not real. That is something we felt very strongly about. That and decorating Christmas cookies.

CHRISTMAS COOKIES

INGREDIENTS

2 cups all-purpose flour (you don't need expensive stuff, these cookies are mostly for looks anyway)

1/2 teaspoon baking powder

Large pinch kosher salt

1 cup granulated sugar

1 stick butter

1 egg

1 teaspoon vanilla extract

2 tablespoons milk

Store-bought buttercream frosting, because this is more about crafting than it is about cooking

1. Determine whether you want to host a cookie-decorating party for adults or for children. Both are equally fun! Just in different ways. Cleanup is about the same.

2. Making sugar cookie dough is pretty simple. In one bowl, add your dry ingredients (flour, baking powder, salt).

3. In another bowl, roughly combine your sugar with your butter. Then add your egg and vanilla, and if you're feeling it, maybe a splash of milk. Experiment!

4. Refrigerate your dough. Make a cocktail! Discuss how much shopping you have left to do!

5. Roll out your dough and cut the cookies into clever shapes. Look at you go! So domestic and intentional.

6. Bake your cookies at 350 degrees for about 10 minutes, and let the cookies cool down before spreading your frosting on top.

7. THIS IS WHERE THINGS GET CREATIVE! Make your home into an edible craft store and tell your guests to have at it. Allow them to express their inner creativity. If they don't have any, then encourage them to just make whatever comes to mind. (Save those cookies so later you can psychoanalyze their meanings.)

Last but not least, pull your child aside and make a Santa with them. When they ask about the "real Santa," tell them to look at the cookie. Teach them that magic is real, and real magic is what we make it. The marvel of the human experience is creation itself. To form something out of nothing. To share common myths. There's so much magic in that: Community *is* creation.

{THEN BITE OFF SANTA'S HEAD.}

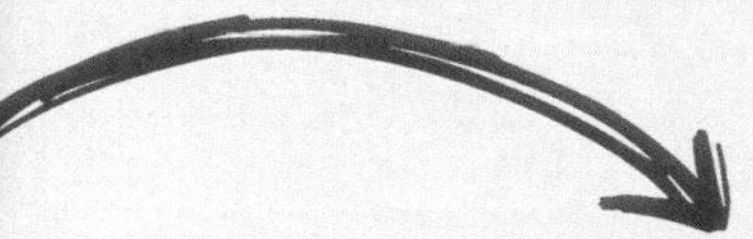

HANUKKAH: STARTS ON THE 25TH DAY OF KISLEV, USUALLY BUT NOT ALWAYS IN DECEMBER

MAZEL, MAZEL, MOTHERFUCKER!

My relationship with Judaism is . . . complicated.* My mother converted to marry my father, but then they both left Judaism to become Jehovah's Witnesses. Eventually they got divorced, and my mother chose to raise us with a theological approach to all religion. Now, she's a Methodist like her grandma used to be. It's been a journey!

As a non-Jew with a Jewish family, community is a funny place to navigate. When I make friends, they tend to be Jewish. If I mention that half of my family is Jewish and my cousins live in Israel, (Jewish) people usually say something like "I knew it!"

I skipped going to Birthright (a free trip to Israel for anyone of Jewish descent until the age of twenty-six), and because of it, Ella likes to constantly remind me that "We could have been Jewish!" Something that she, as a recovering Catholic, would have loved.

* Then again . . . whose isn't!

So why have I chosen to ignore this part of my heritage? Does it stem from a hesitation toward all religion in general? Partially. But mostly it's because I don't want to be something I'm not.

I wish I could lay claim to the cultural and social heritage that comes with it . . . but at the end of the day . . . I'm not Jewish. I'm not even technically "half Jewish" (because of the whole "bloodline of the mother" thing). Do I speak a little Hebrew? Yes, but that's just because of my cousins. If I had been raised in a temple, would I have become a rabbi? Honestly, probably.

But as life panned out for me, at most I would say that I'm Jew-adjacent. Jewjacent? Jew . . . ish?

I'd love to raise our kids with a sense of spirituality. I don't know how we'll get there, but it's something I'd like to explore. At this point in time, though, the most I can hope for is to teach them everything I've learned.

The highlight of all being . . . how to make a decent latke.

LOVE THE WAY YOU LATKE

INGREDIENTS

Russet potatoes (these are the brown ones!)

Onion

Egg

Salt

Avocado oil (or another oil with a high smoke point)

1. Start from starch! Roughly grate your potatez (pronounced: poh-TAY-tuz).

2. Chippity-chop up your onion.

3. Spread all your goodies out, and use a towel to soak up extra moisture. You can do this by twisting or by smooshing. A fun job for a kid!

4. Put your potato blend in a bowl and beat in an egg. And a *tiny* bit of salt. If you're of Jewish or Eastern European descent, then you

are probably prone to anxiety and some form of hypertension, so . . . be gentle with the salt. You can always add more later. Put some lox on your latke after you fry it! Boom! Both salt *and* omegas!

5. Heat up your oil and start sizzling. Depending on how you like your latkes, you can either add them as a hearty dollop or (like me) hand pat them to a flatter shape for maximum sizzle.

6. Accompany with any of your favorite accoutrement and enjoy!

Coming from a blended family, it might be hard to feel welcome during any cultural practice. Even if you do have an emotional connection to multiple practices. I'll never call a latke a potato pancake, because that's just not me.

I can't tell you how to live your life, but I can share how I've chosen to live mine. My personal Festivus would include both latkes and Christmas cookies (not served at the same time, though). Anyone who has a problem with that . . . probably is projecting, so just ignore it and move on. We've got more celebrating to do!

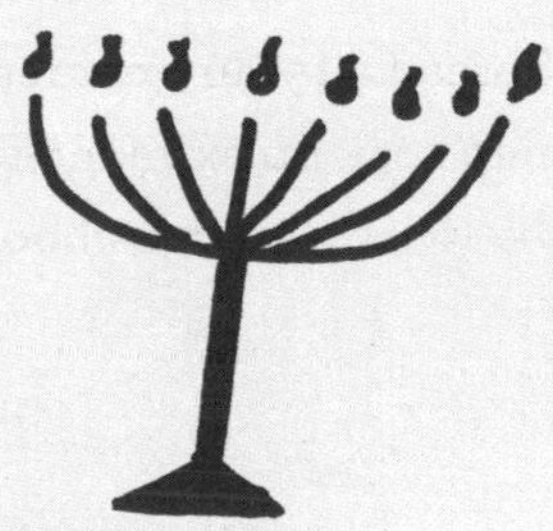

WINTER SOLSTICE: 12/21

WHEN I WAS BORN, I WAS THE YOUNGEST OF TWO GIRLS. When I turned eleven, I was the middle of three girls. At seventeen, I became the middle of five—both boys and girls. Confused? Allow me to very briefly explain. Through adoption, my family has merged into a family of five siblings. I have two older siblings and two younger siblings. Boys and girls on both sides—not that gender makes much of a difference.

When we started celebrating the holidays together as a larger family, it was a bit of a rocky start. Each set of siblings had their own sibling dynamics, and then those sets had dynamics within the larger group. Each individual had their own relationships with each other and so on and so forth. I didn't call the boys (now men) my "brothers" until recently. Though they always called me their sister, there was something that held me back. Maybe it was because I'd never had brothers before. Maybe it was because I was used to being the *leader* of a dysfunctional family as opposed to a *member* of a functional one.

These days it's very easy to be together as a family. In fact, the time we spend all together is my favorite throughout the year. We love to play games, we love to debate, we love to forgive. Three of the five of us (I'm leaving things ambiguous, because they will all be reading this book—hi, guys!!) love to cook. All of us love to eat. Some of us love to drink. Some of us love to smoke. Some of us love to get stomach pains and need to be alone until they go away. One of us has type 1 diabetes. It's a mishmash.

But when we all come together it feels natural. Right. It feels like love. It feels like family.

We are at the start of our new traditions. I'm excited for us to be "the adults" in the dynamic. I'm excited for us all to have children and for those children to be cousins. I'm excited to be gathered together around the TV watching all our family Christmas classics one right after another. (My personal favorite is *The Muppet Christmas Carol*—but some years I can't bear watching it because it overwhelms me with nostalgia and I'd rather busy myself with cooking or errands than succumb to the wave of pure Christmas emotion.)

The next recipe I want to share with you all comes from years of Christmas traditions—the tradition of not talking to one another and just enjoying one another. Not the mealtime but the snack time. The sit back, shut up, and be together time that comes with crowding around our twenty-first-century version of the hearth: the TV.

COZY CORN

INGREDIENTS

Popcorn kernels

Oil

Sugar

Peanuts

Red Hots (or some hot, red candy)

Rosemary

Parmesan

Salt

Pepper

Two separate serving bowls

1. Take a deep breath. You're in the middle of the holiday celebration and it's time for some peace and quiet. Suggest watching some movies so you can excuse yourself to the kitchen to make movie-watching snacks. Drink some water and remember that despite how annoying everyone is, there's nowhere else in the world you'd rather be.

2. Okay! Now it's snack time. You can't please everyone, so best to just make two things that are similar enough to be served simultaneously but different enough to meet everyone's tastes.

3. Put a bunch of popcorn kernels inside a pot of hot oil. Wait for popping.

4. While you're waiting for popping, start to prep your two popcorn options for those loud, whiny people whom you love. Everyone has opinions about everything. As do you.

5. Cozy Corn, the first: Sugarcoat some peanuts tossed together with some Red Hots. Then mix together with half your popcorn batch. This is mostly for "Christmas" looks and for the kids—and grandparents who like to eat unhealthy because, well, why not? Swallow your opinions and concerns.

6. Cozy Corn, the second: Take your second half of freshly popped corn and add some briefly baked rosemary (approximately 300 degrees, keep an eye on it), Parmesan,

salt, and pepper. This is for the grown-ups whom you want to impress. The in-laws and your cockier siblings will have no choice but to compliment your masterful popcorn preparation! They may compliment it silently, though. By just eating all of it and then teasing that next time you should make more. That's how they show their love.

7. Get cozy and make someone else do the dishes.

8. ...

9. ...

10. Get up and do the dishes.

I'd like to tell you who I am in my sibling dynamic: I'm bossy and anxious. I like plans and I like to make sure that everyone has what they need. I have a hard time delegating because I want things to run on my timeline. I'm loving and loved. I appreciate and feel appreciated. I am in the middle of five, and there is nowhere else I'd rather be.

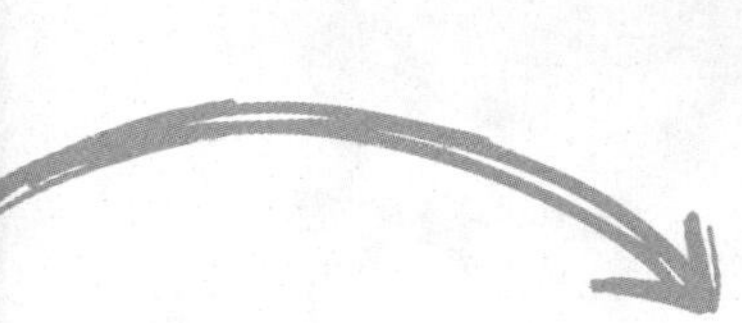

CHAMPAGNE DAY: 12/31

AT LAST WE HAVE ARRIVED TO OUR FINAL DAY OF CELEBRATION. At least our final day of celebration for this year. I hope that as you've read this book, you've been able to digest the year that has passed to make room for the year yet to come. No emotional constipation here! We have celebrated within the fiber-heavy fabric of life.

We have a phrase in our tiny household of two (two cats, two ladies): "Don't Save Champagne." We say it to each other when we are hesitant to allow ourselves joy. Or when worry clouds what could potentially be a good thing. Or when someone brings over a bottle of nice Champagne and encourages us to save it instead of sharing it with them. Pfft. Yeah, right. We're gonna pop that bottle the moment it hits our hot little hands. (Within reason. It might be a Tuesday.)

"Don't Save Champagne" means more than just the literal. Of course, you can't save a bottle once it's been popped; it'll only lose its carbonation, and each subsequent glass will carry with it less and less cause for celebration. This is kind of like being hesitant when receiving good news. That's my default. I greet most things with skepticism, and then I miss out on the joy of hope and opportunity. My mother always told us: "So long as you are breathing, anything is possible." This phrase helped me push through many hours, days, sometimes months of despair.

As long as we continue to be open and awake, we offer ourselves as agents of change. Sometimes in our lives, sometimes in the lives of others. You exist. Though it may not always feel that way, awareness of this fact alone can bring you some measure of joy if you let it. For some of us, it's more difficult to process joy than sorrow. For some of us, good news can lead to the worry of heartbreak. The joy of having and the fear of losing can be dangerously intertwined, so it's our way to remind each other to allow the joy to come when it comes. To celebrate.

And what is celebration, really? Well, in a lot of ways, celebration is an exercise in vulnerability. To celebrate, you have to let your guard down. It's a time of reasonable abandon. To celebrate is to show and share with others exactly how you're feeling. To let them bear witness to something that you've loved or something that you hold dear. To say, "These are the things in life that bring me the greatest sense of joy"—let's celebrate them.

Which is why I'd like to end this book with some simple steps for celebrating all year round. Holidays or not. A holiday is the social permission of celebration. Try and remember there is something to celebrate every day. An easy task? No. But here are some ways to check:

HOW TO NOT SAVE CHAMPAGNE

1. RECEIVE A BOTTLE OF BUBBLY FROM A LOVED ONE. SOMETIMES THAT LOVED ONE IS THE CLERK AT THE STORE WHO SOLD YOU THE BOTTLE. THANKS, BUDDY!

2. HEAD HOME AND CHECK OUT HOW MANY PEOPLE THERE ARE IN THE WORLD AROUND YOU. THEY ALL HAVE DIFFERENT STORIES, DIFFERENT FAMILIES, DIFFERENT LIVES, BUT THEY ALL SHARE THIS SAME MOMENT WITH YOU. ALL THE FACTORS OF THE UNIVERSE CAME TOGETHER AND YOU EXIST IN TANDEM WITH THEM.

3. ASSUME EVERYONE IS DOING THE BEST THEY CAN. THIS THOUGHT ALONE IS CAUSE FOR CELEBRATION.

4. ONCE YOU'RE HOME, PAUSE FOR A MOMENT OF REFLECTION. WRITE A BEAUTIFUL POEM ABOUT EFFERVESCENCE AND HOW OUR SHARED HUMANITY IS LIKE BUBBLES BURSTING ON THE SURFACE OF WATER. CONSTANT BUT EVER CHANGING.

5. DECIDE TO LIVE YOUR LIFE IN THE MOMENT. IF CHAMPAGNE HAS FOUND ITS WAY INTO YOUR HANDS, CELEBRATE THE JOY OF ITS COMING. KISS YOUR WIFE/LOVER/HUSBAND/PARTNER/CAT/DOG/WHATEVER, AND WHEN THEY ASK WHAT WE ARE CELEBRATING, STARE DEEPLY INTO THEIR EYES AND SAY . . . "WE ARE CELEBRATING BECAUSE WE CAN. THAT ALONE IS CAUSE FOR CELEBRATION."

So, cheers to you, my friend! Cheers to this day and to all days! There is always something worth celebrating as long as you look for it. And if your life seems completely devoid of joy, then look to the world around you and try to share in its joy. You are one of many stories. You are never alone.

ACKNOWLEDGMENTS

This book wouldn't be possible without the patience and support of the following people: Jill, Linnea, Brandi, Ella, Fabienne, and everyone unfortunate enough to cross my path while I was trying to write. Thanks so much to everyone who helped with the book's design and production as well, including Lorie, Tiffany, LeeAnn, Dora, and Marya. Also, a major thank-you to Nora for being a badass food stylist—thanks for having fun with me and being game to play.

ABOUT THE AUTHOR

HANNAH HART is an entertainer, food enthusiast, and two-time *New York Times* bestselling author (*Buffering: Unshared Tales of a Life Fully Loaded* and *My Drunk Kitchen: A Guide to Eating, Drinking, and Going with Your Gut*). Since creating the YouTube series *My Drunk Kitchen,* Hart has co-produced and starred in multiple films and hosted her own show on the Food Network, *I Hart Food.* In 2018, Hart launched *Hannahlyze This,* the self-help podcast that just can't help itself. She currently produces and hosts Tasty's *Edible History* on Facebook. Hart's consistent authenticity in her content has established her as one of the most influential voices in the LGBTQ community and gained her recognition as one of *Hollywood Reporter*'s New Digital Disruptors and one of *Forbes'* 30 Under 30. Born and raised in Northern California, Hannah currently resides in Los Angeles with her fiancée and two cats.